FOOD ESSENTIALS

VEGETABLES

FOOD ESSENTIALS
VEGETABLES
BY OLWEN WOODIER

PHOTOGRAPHY BY DAN WILBY

Prop Stylist—Lynn McMahill
Food Stylist—Rebecca Adams

Friedman Group

A FRIEDMAN GROUP BOOK

Copyright © 1993 by Michael Friedman Publishing Group, Inc.
Photographs © 1992 Dan Wilby

ISBN 0-517-06118-X

FOOD ESSENTIALS: VEGETABLES
was prepared and produced by
Michael Friedman Publishing Group, Inc.
15 West 26th Street
New York, New York 10010

Editor: Suzanne DeRouen
Art Director: Jeff Batzli
Photography Editor: Anne Price
Layout: Beverly Bergman
Production: Jeanne E. Kaufman

Typeset by Trufont Typographers, Inc.
Color separations by Rainbow Graphic Arts Co., Ltd.
Printed and bound in Hong Kong by Leefung-Asco Printers Ltd.

 # CONTENTS

"Preserve a good constitution of body and mind. To this a spare diet contributes much. Have wholesome, but no costly food."

William Penn
Some Fruits of Solitude, 1693

DEDICATION
To Helen Nearing, who wrote in *Simple Food for the Good Life*: "Greens are the real staff of life. . . . Vegetation is the universal food, providing us directly or indirectly with all the food we eat. . . ."

ACKNOWLEDGMENTS
A big thanks to all the vegetable associations who sent me their literature so quickly and then responded to my many questions. I'd also like to thank Carol Spier, who has been a great friend and bouncing board for so many years. Last, but certainly not the least, thanks go to Karla Olson for her sound direction and good advice.

There are those people who are natural cooks, and those who quake at the idea of preparing anything more complex than scrambled eggs on toast. The former tend to be creative in the kitchen, and are always on the lookout for both new ideas and basic culinary knowledge that will allow them to follow a whim with a certain guarantee of success; the latter rarely reach beyond the tried-and-true without a cookbook in hand. The former may eschew measuring spoons in favor of "season to taste," while the latter ponder level versus heaping. Both will find guidance and inspiration in the *Food Essentials* series.

Topically organized, these volumes contain the basics of food preparation in an accessible and straightforward format.

But they are much more than convenient, alphabetized indexes of what-is-it-called and how-do-you-cook-it. The *Food Essentials* volumes address all of the culinary needs of today's cook, explaining not only the elemental aspects of buying, storage, and preparation, but the nutritional role played by each of the various foods. The contemporary attitude expressed throughout is one of good health through good food with as little trouble as possible; the diversity of the recipes is unified by common-sense nutrition, fresh ingredients simply but delightfully seasoned, and ease of preparation. The text is sprinkled with bits of food history and countless suggestions for seasoning variations. Both timid and adventurous cooks will be rewarded with every reading of these essential volumes.

Eating the right foods not only keeps us healthy, it also boosts our energy levels and lifts our spirits. Doctors and nutritionists say that we should eat high-fiber foods that are rich in vitamins A and C—fruits and vegetables—something our mothers and grandmothers always told us to do. Now we can choose from an assortment of vegetables that our grandmothers never even knew existed (the ones rich in vitamins A and/or C have been familiar for centuries). They include white and sweet potatoes, carrots, winter squash, peppers, cabbage, broccoli, kale, brussels sprouts, and other leafy green vegetables.

Whether it's during the dog days of summer or when Jack Frost is nipping at our noses, vegetables are always abundant. Today we can get them from all corners of the globe, but if we want to enjoy super-fresh quality, we're better off getting local, home-grown, seasonal vegetables. Since the late eighties, boosted by consumer demand, *certified* organic produce has become available. And many of us are developing into weekend farmers or, at the very least, seeking out the fresh vegetables at farmers markets or supermarkets and health-food stores that have a quick turnover of fresh and, with luck, organically grown produce.

Nothing heralds spring more than the dark green leaves of tender young spinach or the bright green stalks of new asparagus. In summertime, there is the delight of munching on vine-ripened tomatoes and sweet corn picked fresh that morning from a neighboring farm. And think of those crunchy peas and snap beans—bright green, smooth and satiny, unblemished by time—almost a different breed from the dull, out-of-season ones available in supermarkets.

When autumn touches the landscape, choose the sweet and starchy root vegetables, winter squash, and the post-frost greens that are as fresh as a wagon ride away. Or select seasonal vegetables that were grown close enough to be trucked across state and county lines rather than across continents. Autumn vegetables tempt not only with their flavor and texture, but with their vivid greens, purples, and bright oranges. Long pearly white leeks glisten against large, round, deep purple beets. Dark green brussels sprouts vie for attention next to earthy brown mushrooms.

For health reasons, there is a growing trend to replace meat with plant food. For example, the focal point of a meal may be a dish composed of vegetables and grains, pasta, or legumes. A well-balanced diet includes at least three servings of vegetables a day (one-half cup, raw or cooked, is considered one serving). One easy way is to serve up a salad prepared with a variety of thinly sliced, raw vegetables that are in season. Add a baked, boiled, or sautéed potato dish and you've got it made. A bright red sweet pepper or a large summer tomato stuffed with corn, lima beans, and parsley is another efficient way to get your daily ration. You can also serve squash or sweet or white potatoes stuffed with broccoli, mushrooms, asparagus tips, or any of a wide variety of vegetable delights.

Because cooking dinner, at least during the week, is sometimes a matter of juggling priorities, and because stretching one's time has become a daily workout, the recipes in this book have been designed to be quick and easy, for the most part.

I also cook with very little fat. The combination of eating more vegetables and cutting down on fat just makes good sense, if only to meet the new dietary guidelines recommended by many major health associations. A diet low in fat and high in fiber helps keeps your cholesterol levels low and also reduces your risk of cancer. However, if you prefer a richer flavor or thicker texture, by all means substitute butter for margarine or olive oil, cream for low-fat milk, or full-fat cheese for reduced-fat varieties. Doing so will not sabotage the recipes; only your waistline will suffer.

You'll find a wide variety of dishes to choose from, including side dishes, salads, main meals, soups, appetizers, and a few desserts. Enjoy!

KEEPING VEGETABLES RICH IN NUTRIENTS

After taking time to grow and harvest, or pick and choose vegetables in peak condition, there are still a dozen ways to safeguard their nutrients. Here's how:

1. Vegetables are excellent sources of vitamins, but make sure they are brightly colored, not faded or yellowing.

2. Fresh, raw vegetables are best, but frozen ones retain more nutrients than canned ones. In fact, commercially frozen vegetables are processed in perfect condition and are better than old fresh vegetables.

3. Blanch fresh vegetables in boiling water before freezing. Although this destroys some of the vitamin B and C content, it also stops enzyme activity that causes an even greater loss.

4. Freeze vegetables quickly and pack into airtight bags or containers.

5. Keep fresh vegetables as short a time as possible, and store them in a dark environment—a cupboard, refrigerator, or a Styrofoam picnic chest. Bright light depletes the vitamin content and causes potatoes to develop a green toxin in the skin.

6. Retard vitamin loss by storing correctly. Read recommendations for each vegetable in this book.

7. If you *must* wash vegetables before you store them, drain or blot away moisture to avoid rapid deterioration.

8. Don't prepeel, prechop, or presoak vegetables. Vitamins B and C and iron are water soluble and leach out. In fact, try not to peel vegetables at all, because it removes many of the nutrients located under the skin. Just scrub away the dirt and cut out the stem or blossom ends.

9. Raw produce has the highest vitamin content; overcooking destroys nutrients.

10. Pressure cooking, steaming, and microwave cooking reduce the loss of vitamins, because cooking times are shorter than with boiling and less water is used. Aluminum steamers cook faster than bamboo steamers.

11. Vegetables should be boiled until just tender. Shorten cooking times by dropping the vegetables into boiling water and covering the pot. Use just enough water to cover the vegetables.

12. Do not add bicarbonate of soda to vegetables; this destroys vitamins B_1 (thiamin) and C.

13. Choose stainless steel or aluminum pans over copper when cooking vegetables rich in vitamin C.

14. Use a sharp knife when cutting or chopping. A blunt knife tears at the fibers, and vitamin C is lost from bruised vegetables.

15. Save the outer leaves of greens and the peelings from other vegetables (if not treated with chemical pesticides) and add to soups and sauces or make into a nutrient-rich vegetable stock.

VEGETABLE VITAMINS AND MINERALS

According to the National Cancer Institute, a healthy diet includes three half-cup servings of vegetables every day, especially those high in vitamins A and C. Particularly recommended are the cruciferous (mustard family) vegetables, such as cabbage, broccoli, cauliflower, brussels sprouts, kale, collards, turnips, plus other dark green leafy veggies like spinach, chard, and beet greens. These contain beta-carotene, the natural form of vitamin A. Many red, orange, and yellow vegetables, such as peppers, carrots, winter squash, and pumpkins, are also rich in beta and other carotenes. To see which vegetables keep your immune system working in tip-top shape, consult the following chart and find those with the highest concentration of vitamins and minerals.

Folacin (folate, folic acid)	Asparagus, brussels sprouts, turnip greens
Calcium	Beet greens, bok choy, broccoli, collards, kale, scallions, spinach, turnip greens
Iron	Beet greens, dried beans, peas, mushrooms, pumpkin seeds, soybeans, spinach, sunflower seeds
Magnesium	Beet greens, broccoli, dried beans, spinach
Potassium	Artichoke, beet root and greens, broccoli,

brussels sprouts, cabbage, cauliflower, dried beans, kohlrabi, okra, parsnip (salsify), peas, potato, pumpkin (also, leaves and seeds), rutabaga, scallions, spinach, sunflower seeds, sweet potato (also, leaves and skin), winter squash, tomato

Vitamin A Beet greens, bok choy, broccoli, brussels sprouts, carrots, chard, collards, corn, dark green cabbages, French (green) beans, kale, lima beans, peas, pumpkin, spinach, sweet potato, turnip greens, winter squash

Vitamin C Artichokes, asparagus, beet greens, bok choy, broccoli, brussels sprouts, cabbage, collards, cauliflower, green and yellow snap beans, hot and sweet peppers, kale, kohlrabi, lima beans, parsnip, peas, potato with skin, rutabaga, scallions, spinach, sweet potato, tomato, turnip root and greens, winter squash

ARTICHOKE

The globe, or French, artichoke is the immature flower bud of a cultivated thistle. Before the flower has a chance to bloom, it is cut off the plant as a tight, green ball of fleshy (and sometimes prickly) scales. Native to northern Africa, this unusual perennial was grown in Mediterranean countries during Roman times. After the fall of the Roman Empire, the artichoke disappeared, only to experience a renaissance in Italy during the 1400s. By the mid-sixteenth century, its cultivation had spread into France and Great Britain. Although the artichoke was brought to North America by French and Spanish settlers in the 1800s, it was not until a wave of Greek and Italian immigrants brought their love of the artichoke with them in the early 1900s that it developed into a major crop in Castroville, California, now known as the "artichoke center of the world."

Globe artichoke

NUTRITIONAL VALUE

One large artichoke is high in potassium and is a good source of vitamin C, folic acid, magnesium, and phosphorus. It also provides calcium and iron.

BUYING AND STORING

Artichokes are available year-round, with the season peaking in March, April, and May. In the winter and spring months, choose artichokes with firm, tight heads. Winter artichokes touched by frost will have bronze-colored leaves. Summer artichokes have a somewhat conical and flared shape. Artichoke varieties vary at maturity from baby to jumbo—pick the ones heaviest for their size, for they will have the meatiest leaves and base. The latest types are thornless and red, with meatier leaves and larger hearts. Large artichokes are good for boiling, steaming, and stuffing. The smaller tender ones are a better choice for sautéeing, marinating, and combining in casseroles.

Store fresh artichokes in a plastic bag in the refrigerator for up to a week.

Artichoke hearts and bottoms are available frozen or canned in brine or oil.

PREPARATION

The base of each leaf and the heart of the artichoke attached to the stem are the only parts that are edible. The fuzzy "choke" in the center and the rest of the leaves are not edible except in baby artichokes. The mature baby artichokes are not as tender and must still be trimmed and cleaned.

Vary Artichoke Risotto by substituting artichoke bottoms cut in quarters for the hearts and bay scallops for the shrimp.

To clean: cut off the stem (level with the bottom) and about 1 inch off the top leaves. If the bottom leaves are dry, snap them off. If desired, trim ¼ inch off each of the remaining leaves.

Spread open the leaves and pull out the purplish, prickly center. Scrape out the "choke" at this stage or leave until cooked, when it is easier to remove with a spoon.

Rinse the artichoke and squeeze lemon juice over the cut leaves and in the center.

To cook: artichokes can be boiled, steamed, braised, or baked; by any method, cooking will require approximately 30 minutes. To cut the time in half, cook in a microwave or pressure cooker. Set the prepared artichokes upright in a stainless steel or enamel pan. Add 2 to 3 inches of water and the juice of one lemon. Cover and bring to a boil. Reduce the heat to medium and simmer until done. Drain the artichokes upside down. Stuff the cooked artichokes or serve with a sauce. To eat, pull off each leaf and dip the base into a sauce. Draw the fleshy part through the teeth. Continue until all the leaves have been removed. Scrape away the fuzzy choke, if necessary, and cut the heart into bite-size pieces. Dip into a sauce and enjoy.

To cook the heart only, trim off the stem and remove all the leaves and the fuzzy choke. Leave whole or cut in half. Sauté, braise, or microwave with garlic and oil. Use as a side dish or puree for use in a soup or soufflé.

Artichoke Risotto

2	*tablespoons olive oil*
1	*medium onion, chopped*
2	*cloves garlic, finely minced*
½	*cup sliced mushrooms*
1	*cup Arborio rice*
2½	*cups vegetable stock or water plus a bouillon cube*
1	*1-pound can artichoke hearts, drained and quartered (reserve liquid for the vegetable stock)*
1	*pound shrimp, shelled, cleaned, and cut in half*
	Salt and pepper to taste
2	*tablespoons chopped fresh parsley*
6	*cherry tomatoes, quartered*
½	*cup Parmesan cheese*

Heat the oil in a large skillet over medium heat. Add the onion and sauté 5 minutes. Add the garlic and mushrooms and sauté 2 minutes. Stir in the rice. When glistening with oil, add 1 cup of the vegetable stock. Stir until the rice absorbs the liquid. Reduce the heat to low and slowly add a second cup of liquid. Cook until absorbed before adding the final half-cup. Stir in the artichoke hearts and shrimp. Cook 5 minutes until the shrimp are pink, just cooked through, and hot. Remove to a serving dish. Season with the salt and pepper and stir in the parsley, quartered cherry tomatoes, and Parmesan cheese. Serve immediately.

Note: Save time with this recipe by stirring leftover cooked rice into the sautéed onions and mushrooms with only ½ cup liquid.

Preparation time: 20 minutes
Cooking time: 35 minutes
Yield: 4 servings

Tomato-Stuffed Artichokes with Basil Sauce

4   *large artichokes, stems and tough outer leaves removed*
      Juice of 1 lemon
1   *tablespoon olive oil*
4   *scallions, thinly sliced*
2   *cloves garlic, finely minced*
½   *cup pine nuts*
2   *large tomatoes, peeled, seeded, and diced*
1½   *cups dry bread crumbs*
¼   *cup chopped fresh parsley*
½   *cup grated Parmesan cheese*
      Salt and pepper to taste

Trim 1 inch off the top leaves of the artichokes and snip off the points from the rest. Rub the cut edges with lemon juice. Place the artichokes, stem side down, in a small dish with ¼ cup water. Cover with plastic wrap and microwave on high for 10 minutes. Allow the artichokes to cool. In the meantime, prepare the stuffing. Heat the oil in a skillet over medium heat and sauté the scallions, garlic, and pine nuts for 2 minutes. Remove from heat. Stir in the tomatoes, bread crumbs, parsley, parmesan cheese, salt and pepper. When the artichokes are cool enough to handle, press open the leaves from the center and pull out the inner pink cone. Using a small spoon, scoop out the fuzzy choke. Spoon the stuffing into the centers and between each of the outer leaves. Return the artichokes to the microwave dish, add ¼ cup water, and cover tightly with plastic wrap. Microwave on high for 10 minutes. Serve warm with Basil Sauce.

Note: Don't forget to remove the prickly inner choke. You can get more stuffing into the artichokes, and it makes them easier to eat.

Preparation time: 30 minutes
Cooking time: 20 minutes
Yield: 4 servings

Basil Sauce

1   *cup low-fat mayonnaise*
2   *tablespoons lemon juice*
1   *clove garlic*
½   *cup fresh basil leaves*

Place all the ingredients in a blender or food processor and process until smooth. Serve in little bowls alongside the artichokes. Remove the outer leaves and dip in the sauce. Use a knife and fork to cut the artichoke heart into bite-size pieces. Dip into the sauce and enjoy!

JERUSALEM ARTICHOKE
HELIANTHUS TUBEROSUS

The Jerusalem artichoke is the root end of a plant which bears several stalks topped with small heads of yellow sunflowers. The "sunchoke," as it is also called, grows wild, turning fields and hedgerows yellow during late summer and early autumn. Native Americans cultivated sunflower plants for seeds, yellow dye, fibrous stalks, and the edible roots of some species. The edible tuber plants were introduced into Europe during the seventeenth century.

Although several varieties are available to the home gardener, the purveyor of specialty vegetables may find only two: golden brown tubers with creamy white flesh or those that are tinged with pink. The tubers are about the size of narrow new potatoes. The nutty-flavored raw flesh is crisp and thin slices make a crunchy addition to a salad.

NUTRITIONAL VALUE
A half-cup of raw slices provides minor levels of calcium and vitamins A and C. However, the protein supplied is 1.5 grams, slightly more than ½ cup of baked potato without the skin.

BUYING AND STORING
Buy firm, unblemished tubers and refrigerate in a plastic bag for up to two weeks. Available for several months of the year, the sweetest are those sold in autumn and winter. Store-bought sunchokes can be planted in the garden.

PREPARATION
Fresh Jerusalem artichokes can be scrubbed, sliced, and tossed with lemon

juice to prevent a brown discoloration. Serve raw slices in a salad or stir-fry them in Oriental dishes. Steam whole chokes on top of the stove or in a microwave for 10 to 15 minutes. Older tubers may need to be peeled before boiling and mashing or adding to soups.

Sunchokes Provençale

Serve this fast and easy sauce over pasta or rice. It also makes a flavorful side dish.

1	tablespoon olive oil
1	large red onion, chopped (about 1 cup)
3	cloves garlic, minced
1½	pounds Jerusalem artichokes, scrubbed and cut in ½-inch cubes
1	cup pitted black olives, cut in half
4	medium ripe or canned tomatoes, chopped (about 1⅓ cups)
1	tablespoon fresh thyme leaves or 1 teaspoon dried
	Salt and pepper to taste

Heat the oil in a large skillet over medium heat and sauté the onion and garlic for 5 minutes. Add the sunchoke cubes, stir, and cook 2 minutes before adding the olives, chopped tomatoes, thyme, and salt and pepper. Cover tightly, reduce the heat to low, and cook for 10 to 15 minutes, until the sunchokes are tender. Serve hot or at room temperature.

Jerusalem Artichoke Relish

Because this is a relish, the vegetables are barely cooked. For this reason, it is necessary to process them in a boiling-water bath.

2	pounds Jerusalem artichokes, trimmed and scrubbed
1	pound carrots, trimmed and peeled (or scrubbed)
1	large yellow onion
3	cups vinegar
1	tablespoon kosher salt
1	tablespoon pickling spice
1	teaspoon crushed red pepper
1	cup brown sugar

Bring a large pot of water to a boil and cook the artichokes for 1 minute. Remove with a slotted spoon into a colander and rinse under cold water. Drain, blot dry, and coarsely chop. Place in a mixing bowl. Use the same boiling water for the carrots and cook for 2 minutes. Remove and rinse under cold running water. Drain, blot dry, coarsely chop, and add to the bowl. Coarsely chop the onion and add to the artichoke mixture. In a 4-quart stainless steel or enamel saucepan, bring the vinegar, salt, pickling spice, crushed red pepper, and brown sugar to a boil over high heat, stirring to dissolve the sugar, 3 to 5 minutes. Add the chopped vegetables and return to a rolling boil. Spoon into hot, clean glass jars. Run a knife around the inside of the jars to remove air bubbles, wipe the rims clean, and screw down the tops tightly. Process in a submerged boiling-water bath for 10 minutes. Remove with tongs and cool.

Note: To make a chutney that can be stored in the refrigerator, in step 4, simply simmer until most of the liquid has been cooked away and the mixture is thick.

Preparation time: 20 minutes
Cooking time: 16 minutes
Yield: 8 cups

Jerusalem Artichokes are nutty-flavored little roots that add a crunch to salads.

ASPARAGUS

ASPARAGUS OFFICINALIS,
FAMILY LILIACEAE

Native to Europe and cultivated since Roman times, asparagus is a perennial plant grown for its swollen stem (its name is taken from the Greek word meaning "to swell"). There are two main types of asparagus: "French," which produces large and thick, succulent, light green stems (frequently grown without light to achieve white stems barely tinted with light yellow or pale purple) and the thinner, green type that is grown commercially in many countries. For this reason, even though asparagus is essentially a spring crop, it is available from imported sources for several months of the year.

In Europe, asparagus vinaigrette is often served as a first-course treat early in the season. (Asparagus is one of the few foods Europeans find acceptable to eat with the fingers.) Americans seem to prefer young asparagus served as a side dish, lightly dressed with butter or hollandaise sauce. When its price goes down later in the season, there are many other ways to serve asparagus: baked with cheese; creamed for soup; stuffed into crepes, enchiladas, omelettes, and pastry cases; sliced for stir-fries, salads, and pastas; deep-fried in tempura batter; or made into dainty finger sandwiches or served on toast points.

NUTRITIONAL VALUE

Asparagus is a good source of vitamin A and the B vitamins. It is also an excellent source of vitamin C—just four medium-size stalks provide 25 percent of the U.S. Recommended Daily Allowance.

BUYING AND STORING

Out-of-season and thick-stemmed varieties of asparagus are the most expensive. Whether the spears are thick or thin, when fresh they should be firm and smooth with tightly pointed buds. The flavor will be intense and sweet, the texture crisply tender. Flaccid, flat, or wrinkled stems with loose buds indicate old, dried-out asparagus.

Asparagus doesn't store well, so plan on using it within two days of purchase. Refrigerate in a plastic bag in the vegetable drawer or stand in a jar with about an inch of water and cover with a plastic bag. To keep it for a longer period, trim off the lower stems and blanch in boiling water for about 2 minutes. Remove from the heat, run under cold water, drain, and refrigerate in a covered dish or freeze in a sealed bag or container.

Fresh, tender green asparagus spears are a sure harbinger of spring.

PREPARATION

Thin, young asparagus spears are usually tender along the entire length. Don't bother to peel them, just trim a thin slice off the end. Larger, more mature spears will need to be trimmed and peeled to remove the tough skin below the buds.

There are special asparagus cookers on the market. Fitted with a steamer basket, they are designed to cook the spears in a vertical or a horizontal position. When cooking in a pot without a basket, tie the asparagus in bundles for easy removal. Asparagus can also be cooked in a covered skillet. Place the asparagus in a single layer and barely cover with water. Cover the skillet and bring the water to a boil over medium-high heat. Reduce the heat and simmer for 5 minutes or until done.

To microwave, place 12 prepared spears in a dish with the tips facing inward. Add ¼ cup of water, cover with plastic wrap, and cook on high for 5 to 7 minutes.

Asparagus Soup

Serve this soup hot or chilled—it's delicious either way.

2	*pounds asparagus, peeled and cut into 1-inch pieces*
4	*medium potatoes, peeled and diced*
1	*tablespoon vegetable oil, margarine, or butter*
1	*medium yellow onion, chopped (about ¾ cup)*
¼	*cup chopped fresh parsley*
1	*tablespoon fresh lemon thyme leaves or ½ teaspoon dried*
1	*cup low-fat sour cream or plain yogurt*
	Salt and pepper to taste
	Parsley leaves

Bring 5 cups of water to a boil in a 3-quart saucepan. Add the asparagus tips and cook 3 minutes, until just tender. Remove with a slotted spoon to a plate and reserve. Add the asparagus stalks and diced potato to the boiling water, reduce the heat, and cover the pan. Meanwhile, heat the oil in a skillet over medium heat and sauté the onion for 5 minutes. Add to the asparagus stalks and diced potato and simmer for 20 minutes. Remove from the heat and process 2 cups at a time in the food processor with the parsley, thyme, and sour cream. Season with salt and pepper to taste and pour into soup bowls. Garnish with the reserved asparagus tips and parsley leaves.

Preparation time: 20 minutes
Cooking time: 30 minutes
Yield: 4 to 6 servings

Warm Asparagus and Spinach Salad

Serve this salad for a delicious spring lunch with a hearty quick bread or muffins.

1	*tablespoon vegetable oil*
2	*pounds asparagus, peeled and cut into 2-inch diagonal pieces*
1	*clove garlic, crushed*
1	*teaspoon dry mustard*
½	*teaspoon ground ginger*
½	*teaspoon curry powder*
2	*tablespoons balsamic vinegar*
2	*tablespoons water*
6	*tablespoons olive oil*
¾	*pound spinach, washed, stems discarded and leaves torn in half*
4	*hard-boiled eggs, shelled and chopped*

Heat the oil in a skillet over medium heat and add the asparagus pieces. Cover and cook for 5 minutes, shaking the skillet occasionally. Combine the garlic, dry mustard, ginger, curry powder, balsamic vinegar, water, and olive oil in a screw-top jar and shake to combine. Place the spinach in a serving bowl, add the hot asparagus, and immediately pour the salad dressing over. Toss to combine, and sprinkle with the chopped egg.

Preparation time: 15 minutes
Cooking time: 25 minutes
Yield: 4 servings

Asparagus Stir-Fry

1   tablespoon sesame oil
1   tablespoon vegetable oil
2   pounds asparagus, peeled and cut in
    2-inch diagonal pieces
2   cloves garlic, minced or crushed
1   tablespoon finely chopped ginger root
2   tablespoons mild soy sauce
2   tablespoons rice wine
2   tablespoons toasted sesame seeds

Heat the oils in a deep skillet or a wok and stir-fry the asparagus, garlic, and ginger for 4 minutes over medium-high heat. Stir in the soy sauce and rice wine, cover the skillet, and simmer for 2 minutes. Turn into a serving bowl and toss with the sesame seeds. Serve immediately as a side dish, over noodles or rice.

Note: This method leaves the asparagus tender but crisp.

Preparation time: 10 minutes
Cooking time: 5 minutes
Yield: 4 to 6 servings

This quick and easy asparagus stir-fry will be ready in the same amount of time as it takes to boil the pasta.

PHASEOLUS, FAMILY LEGUMINOSAE

Most green beans that are eaten fresh as immature pods or as mature seeds belong to the true bean genus *Phaseolus*. These include French beans, runner beans, lima beans, and bean sprouts, all of which are native to Central and South America.

FRENCH BEAN
PHASEOLUS VULGARIS

Brought from the Americas to Europe at the beginning of the sixteenth century, this bean also goes by many other names: dwarf bean, kidney bean, string bean, snap bean, Bobbi bean, and *haricot vert*. To confuse the matter even further, when the pods are mature and only the fresh beans are eaten, they are called green shell beans and flageolets. Yellow wax and purple beans are colored varieties of French beans. Most varieties of French beans are grown as bush beans, although some are climbing pole beans.

Varieties vary in length at recommended harvesting time from 4 to 12 inches long. Although most have pods that are quite narrow, some are flat and wide, while others are round.

NUTRITIONAL VALUE
Green beans are rich in vitamins A, B, and C, and are also a moderate source of iron, calcium, and protein. Yellow wax beans are not quite as high in protein.

BUYING AND STORING
Some varieties of green beans are available year-round. However, the tenderest, crunchiest, and most flavorful pods are the ones purchased during the local growing season and eaten within hours of being picked. Fresh beans are picked when immature and tender enough to be snapped in half (that's why they're called "snap" beans). Choose those that are a rich color, firm, and unblemished. Young beans have fleshy-walled pods with a glossy sheen. Mature beans lose

that bloom as the seeds get bigger, at which point the pods start to dry out and the texture becomes fibrous.

Store green beans in a plastic bag in the refrigerator for 2 to 4 days. For longer storage in the freezer, wash, trim, and slice beans (or leave whole) and drop into boiling water for 2 to 3 minutes. Remove, plunge into ice-cold water, blot dry, and freeze in airtight plastic bags or containers.

Green shell beans (flageolets) are available in cans.

PREPARATION
Most green (and purple or yellow) beans today are stringless. Trim off the top and the tail if it's particularly long. Cut the beans into 1-inch lengths straight across or on the diagonal. Or, if they are very young and small, leave them whole. (If you're bringing in beans from the garden and they are old and large, shell them and cook them like lima or broad beans.) Beans cook very quickly in a

skillet. Just cover the beans with water salted to taste and bring to a boil over high heat. Reduce the heat to medium-low, cover the skillet, and cook 5 to 7 minutes, until tender but still crunchy. Cook older, tougher beans a little longer, then remove from heat and drop into a basin of cold water to retain their green color. Drain and toss with salad dressing. Another way is to cut the beans in half lengthwise, cook until tender, and drain. Top with grated cheese and broil until cheese is bubbly.

RUNNER BEANS
PHASEOLUS COCCINEUS

When this bean was first brought to Europe in the early seventeenth century, it was prized for its ornamental scarlet flowers, rather than its edible pods. It is still valued today by gardeners who want to attract hummingbirds or decorate a bamboo "wigwam" with a flowering, climbing (pole) plant.

BUYING AND STORING
To enjoy the entire pod, buy the smallest and youngest runner beans, for they become stringy, fibrous, and tough very quickly. For this reason, they do not transport well and are not available year-round. Fresh, tender beans will be bright green and will snap in half easily.

Store runner beans in the refrigerator for 2 to 4 days. For longer storage, freeze young ones like French beans. In the home garden, allow the pods to mature on the plant. Bring indoors, shell, and dry the beans at room temperature. Store in a jar and use as dried beans.

Eat runner beans when they're bright green and snap in half easily. Shell the tougher, older ones or drop them into the soup pot.

PREPARATION
Runner beans possess strings running from the top to the tail. Cut off the top and pull down in one long sweep to remove the string. Fresh tender beans can be cooked like French beans. Slightly older ones will do better in the soup pot. When the pod is too old and tough, shell and cook the beans like limas.

LIMA BEANS
PHASEOLUS LUNATUS

Native to Peru and dating back to prehistoric times, lima beans are perennial in tropical climates. Limas, also called butter beans and Madagascar beans, are grown in North America and Europe as an annual. When immature, they have a green pod with small, pale green or white seeds. Some gardeners harvest limas when they are immature so they can eat the pod, but it is more common to shell mature lima pods and cook the fresh large seeds.

Another bean somewhat similar to the lima is the broad bean (*Vicia faba*), also known as the fava bean and the English bean. Although the entire pod with tiny seeds can be eaten when it is only 2 inches long, it is available in the green markets when it is more mature and the beans have begun to show through the pod. The bright green pods are thick-walled with a soft silver lining that envelops large, tender pale green beans. Like limas, broad beans are usually boiled or steamed, and served with butter and seasonings or in a white parsley sauce. Lima beans are an essential element in succotash, a dish that includes sweet corn and sweet peppers.

NUTRITIONAL VALUE

These beans are nutritional giants, providing not only a high content of protein and vitamins A, B, and C, but a good amount of calcium and iron. They are also an excellent source of fiber.

BUYING AND STORING

Taking anywhere from 75 to 95 days to mature, limas are grown in regions that have long, warm summers. Peak season is late summer into early fall. Fresh limas are sometimes available shelled. If not, look for pods that are firm, smooth, and a fresh green color without dark blemishes. Young beans will show as small swellings through the pod.

Store in a plastic bag in the refrigerator for 2 days.

Look for lima beans in the frozen foods section or among the canned vegetables. They are also available in dried form.

PREPARATION

Shell commercially grown limas and, if necessary, remove the tough skins from large beans. These are sometimes easier to remove once the beans have been cooked for 8 to 10 minutes in a little boiling water. Slit the skin around the edge with a sharp knife and push out the flesh. Once shelled, they can be sautéed in butter. Small, tender beans can be cooked in boiling water for 10 minutes, until tender.

MUNG BEANS
VIGNA RADIATA

Mung beans are native to India, where they are used in soups and curries. Elsewhere, they are commonly eaten in a sprouted form and are particularly associated with Chinese food. The Chinese also make them into a type of noodle called *fen tiao*.

NUTRITIONAL VALUE

Mung bean sprouts provide some protein, moderate amounts of vitamin C, and lots of vitamin B_6.

BUYING AND STORING

Although at one time the freshest shoots were those sprouted in a glass jar on the kitchen counter, today bean sprouts are widely available year-round in the supermarkets and green markets. Buy those that look creamy white and crisp, for they will be the freshest and sweetest. They do not store well, so be sure to refrigerate them in a perforated plastic bag and use within 2 days.

PREPARATION

Bean sprouts make a pleasantly crunchy addition to salads, omelette fillings, stir-fries, and mixed vegetable dishes.

Green Bean and Pasta Salad

This is a delicious dish to take along on a summer picnic.

12 ounces pasta shells
1 pound green snap beans, tops and strings removed, cut in 1-inch pieces
1 pound solid white tuna in spring water
1 cup pitted black olives, cut in half
¼ cup olive oil
½ cup low-fat mayonnaise
¼ cup white wine vinegar or lemon juice
 Salt and pepper to taste
3 cloves garlic, finely minced
1 tablespoon fresh chopped tarragon
2 tablespoons fresh chopped chives

Bring water to a boil in a 3-quart saucepan over high heat. Add pasta and boil for 5 minutes. Add green beans and continue cooking for 5 to 6 minutes longer, until beans and pasta are tender. Drain into a colander and rinse under cold water. Drain thoroughly. Turn into a large mixing bowl and add the tuna and black olives. Combine the olive oil, mayonnaise, vinegar, salt, pepper, and garlic in a small bowl and whisk until smooth. Stir in the tarragon and chives. Pour into the pasta bowl and mix the contents together. Serve warm or chilled.

Preparation time: 15 minutes
Cooking time: 10 minutes
Yield: 4 servings

Lima Bean Medley

Don't wait for summer to make this dish. Use frozen beans and corn and canned tomatoes instead of fresh.

1	tablespoon olive oil
1	large green bell pepper, chopped (about 1 cup)
1	medium onion, chopped (about ¾ cup)
2	cloves garlic, finely minced
2	large ripe or canned tomatoes, pureed (about 1½ cups)
1	cup fresh or frozen lima beans
1	cup fresh or frozen corn kernels
	Salt and pepper to taste
½	cup basil leaves, torn in half

Heat the oil in a large skillet over medium heat. Sauté the bell pepper, garlic, and onion for 5 minutes. Stir in the tomatoes, lower the heat, and simmer for 5 minutes. Add the lima beans and corn kernels, stir to combine, cover the skillet, and simmer for 10 minutes. Remove the cover and stir in the salt, pepper, and basil leaves.

Preparation time: 15 minutes
Cooking time: 20 minutes
Yield: 4 to 6 servings

Lima Bean Medley is high in protein and easy to prepare. Toss it with pasta or grains or serve it with potatoes; it makes a delicious, nutritious meal.

Bean Sprout Omelette

A delicious, easy recipe for breakfast, lunch, or dinner.

2	eggs
1	tablespoon skim milk
	Pepper to taste
1	teaspoon olive oil

Filling

2	tablespoons hot-pepper jelly
2	to **3** slices of a ripe tomato
6	basil leaves, shredded
¼	cup bean sprouts

Beat together the eggs, milk, and pepper. Heat the oil in an 8-inch skillet over medium heat for about 2 minutes until oil is hot. Pour in the egg mixture and tilt the skillet to distribute over the bottom surface. When the egg starts to cling to the bottom, gently draw the sides of the omelette to the center with a fork. Tip the pan so uncooked liquid flows onto the pan surface. Repeat until there is no more liquid. When the top is lightly set, drop teaspoons of the hot-pepper jelly over one half. Top with tomato slices, shredded basil, and bean sprouts. Fold the other half of the omelette over the filling. Slip from the skillet onto a warm plate and serve immediately.

Note: To make an omelette for two people, use a 10-inch skillet and double the recipe. If desired, instead of using 4 whole eggs, use 2 whole and 3 additional egg whites only.

Preparation time: 5 minutes
Cooking time: 5 minutes
Yield: 1 serving

First cultivated in Mediterranean countries from the wild species of *Beta maritima*, the beet was grown by the Greeks and Romans more for its leaves than its roots. Beets sold in the supermarket usually have deep red, round roots attached to bright red stems with dark green leaves. These are called "ball" or "globe" beets. Some market and home gardeners, though, choose to grow varieties that have cylindrical or tapered roots or that are a rich golden orange color. And keep an eye open at the farmers' markets and specialty stores for those that are striped with alternating rings of bright pink and white. There is also an all-white beetroot. The lighter-fleshed roots have a sweeter flavor than the deep red beets, and the leaves are also milder.

NUTRITIONAL VALUE

While the root provides moderate amounts of protein, fiber, calcium, magnesium, phosphorous, folacin, and vitamins A and C, the greens are an excellent source of calcium, iron, potassium, and vitamin A. In fact, one half-cup of cooked greens offers 5,100 IU of vitamin A.

BUYING AND STORING

Easy to grow, with big yields in a short season, beets are available year-round. Peak season for young beets with tender tops is early summer. Leaves and stems that are 4 to 8 inches are the mildest, while the larger, darker greens contain more iron.

While some beet varieties produce finer greens than roots, there is another member of the beet family, Swiss chard, also known as "seakale beet" (*Beta vulgaris* var. *cicla*), that is grown exclusively for its 18-inch-long, broad, white stems and green leaves. A red variety of chard is called rhubarb chard because of its red-green leaves and stems. Chard is available as a fall/winter crop. Remove the leafy part from the stem and use like beet greens or spinach. Use the bland, fleshy stems to add fiber to the soup pot; otherwise, steam or boil and serve *au gratin* or in a seasoned white sauce.

Store fresh beetroots in a plastic bag in the refrigerator for 8 to 10 days or in a cool, dry shed for 4 to 6 days. Keep beet tops and chard enclosed in plastic in the vegetable drawer of the refrigerator for 2 to 3 days.

Whole baby beets and sliced beets are available canned and pickled. Freeze cooked, skinned, and sliced beets for up to 6 months.

PREPARATION

Cut off leaves to within 1 inch of the ball, leave the thin root at the base in-

Both the leaves and the root of the beet are edible.

tact, and wash the roots in cold water. Cutting the skin causes bleeding of color and loss of flavor. Choose beets of the same size so that they cook uniformly. Cover with water and boil for 45 to 60 minutes. Cook them in the microwave in a covered casserole with a half-cup of water for 20 minutes. Cool, remove the stem and root ends, and slide off the skin. Slice, dice, or grate, and serve as a vegetable, in a salad, or covered with a pickling solution.

There are many ways to serve beet roots and their greens. Chop or grate the cooked roots, toss with butter, and serve over a bed of steamed and chopped beet greens. Substitute pureed beet greens for spinach in a cheese souffle, lasagna, quiche, or other recipe. Add shredded or torn leaves to soups and stir-fries. For classic borscht, grate the raw beets into a mixture of onions, celery, carrots, and stock, simmer until tender, and top with a spoonful of sour cream. Combine apple and cooked beet slices and toss in an orange-flavored salad dressing. Stir-fry thinly sliced raw beets with turnip and rutabaga.

Beet and Avocado Salad

1	*pound beet roots, cooked, cooled, skin removed*
2	*medium ripe avocados, pits removed*
1	*tablespoon lemon juice*
	Juice and peel of 1 orange
½	*cup low-fat mayonnaise*
½	*cup nonfat yogurt*
2	*cloves garlic, crushed*

Arrange colorful Beet and Avocado Salad on individual plates and serve as a first course.

Cut the beet roots and avocados into ¼-inch-thick slices. Sprinkle the avocado slices with lemon juice to prevent discoloration. Grate a few long shreds of peel from the orange and reserve for garnishing. Grate the rest of the peel on the small perforated section of grater. In a small bowl, mix this finely grated peel into the mayonnaise and yogurt. Cut the orange in half and squeeze the juice into a measuring jug. Add 2 tablespoons to the mayonnaise mixture and blend until smooth. Stir in the crushed garlic. Spoon the dressing onto a round serving plate. Arrange the beet and avocado slices in alternating circular layers. Garnish with the long shreds of orange peel. Serve chilled or at room temperature.

Preparation time: 15 minutes
Yield: 4 servings

Beet Root Gratiné

This recipe is a tasty alternative to the traditional beets and sour cream.

1½	*pounds beet roots, cooked for 20 minutes in the microwave, skinned, and sliced ¼ inch thick*
⅓	*cup low-fat sour cream*
	Pepper to taste
1	*tablespoon chopped fresh dill*
⅓	*to ½ cup grated Parmesan cheese*

In a medium-size bowl, toss beet slices with sour cream, pepper, and dill. Layer in a shallow baking dish and sprinkle with Parmesan cheese. Place 6 inches under the broiler and broil 3 minutes, until the cheese is golden brown.

Preparation time: 10 minutes
Cooking time: 23 minutes
Yield: 4 servings

BROCCOLI AND CAULIFLOWER

This genus includes not only several varieties of true cabbage—savoy, green, and red (*bok choy* and Chinese are separate species)—but also broccoli and cauliflower, brussels sprouts, kale and collards, and kohlrabi. Most of these leafy vegetables were cultivated during Roman times from wild sea cabbage growing in the Mediterranean regions of Europe. The brussels sprout was developed in Belgium during the eighteenth century. Kohlrabi, a cross between a turnip and cabbage, is of unknown origin.

Brassicas are packed with beta-carotene (also called pro-vitamin A or natural vitamin A), vitamin C, and/or calcium. Beta-carotene and vitamin C have been heralded during recent years as having cancer-blocking qualities that might prevent the formation of tumors.

It's not only the dark green members of the cruciferous family that are the healthiest. Some of the lighter green cabbages are higher in vitamin C, while others are higher in vitamin A. Check the individual nutritional values.

Deep green and crunchy, broccoli is a storehouse of vitamins.

Broccoli
Brassica oleracea var. *italica*

The first written reference to broccoli in Roman times grouped it with cauliflower. Even in the early eighteenth century, it was referred to as "sprout cauliflower." At this time, seeds were sent from Italy to England, where the different types that are grown today originated.

Some broccoli varieties produce large heads, others produce several stems and smaller heads. The large-headed ones resemble cauliflower and, during recent years, a pale green hybrid has been commercially marketed as "broccoflower." The flavor is mild and acceptable to those who don't enjoy the assertive flavor of the multi-stemmed

green "sprouting" or common broccoli. Green broccoli is also called Italian or calabrese, after varieties by those names and the fact that the Italian word for "broccoli" is *calabrese*.

Although not commercially popular, some varieties are white or purple. The whites taste similar to cauliflower, while the purples are more flavorful and turn green when cooked. These broccoli varieties are turning up more often at farmers and specialty green markets.

NUTRITIONAL VALUE
A half-cup, cooked and chopped, provides 1,099 IU vitamin A, 49 mg vitamin C, 127 mg potassium, 89 mg calcium, and 53.3 mcg folacin.

Cauliflower
Brassica oleracea var. *botrytis*
Like broccoli, there are several types of cauliflower that can be grown over a period of months, making them available year-round. Some grown in the cooler months are misnamed and are actually heading broccoli. Most form compact, dense, cream-colored heads, although there is a purple variety, which produces a large central head and smaller side stems like broccoli plants. Although some white cauliflowers are self-blanching varieties, those grown in warmer weather need to have their leaves tied over the developing heads to shield them from the sun.

NUTRITIONAL VALUE
A half-cup, cooked, provides 9 IU vitamin A, 34.3 mg vitamin C, 200 mg potassium, 31.7 mcg folacin, and 17 mg calcium.

The creamy-colored, tight curds of a fresh cauliflower are perfect for blanching and serving with a light yogurt dip or salad dressing.

BUYING AND STORING BROCCOLI AND CAULIFLOWER
Choose cauliflower heads or "curds" that are firm and unblemished. Broccoli should have tight, firm heads. A yellow cast indicates the buds are beginning to flower and the plant is past its prime.

Store cauliflower and broccoli in a plastic bag in the refrigerator for up to 3 days. For long storage, blanch florets in boiling water for 2 minutes, drain, and place in the freezer in airtight containers.

PREPARATION OF CAULIFLOWER AND BROCCOLI
Cauliflower is a little crunchier than broccoli and needs a few minutes more cooking time. Remove the outer leaves and reserve for the soup pot or the compost heap. Separate the individual florets from the main stem and steam in 1 inch of water for 8 to 10 minutes or less. To cook the whole head, cut the stem off close to the florets, cut a cross on the bottom, and steam for 15 minutes, until tender. Serve sprinkled with sautéed bread crumbs; chopped egg; parsley sauce; a mixture of chopped garlic, parsley, and grated lemon peel; or a basil-walnut pesto.

For stir-fry and fritter recipes, blanch the florets in boiling water for 2 to 3 minutes. Drain, blot on a kitchen towel, and slice the florets in half vertically. Then continue with the recipe.

To eat them raw, blanch, drain, and plunge the florets into a bowl of ice water to retain their bright, fresh color. They can now be added to a serving platter with a cheese or herb dip, marinated in an Italian-style, garlicky salad dressing or a sesame-and-soy-flavored sauce, or simply coated with a blue cheese mayonnaise.

You can also use the florets in creamed soups, soufflés, quiches, casseroles, and pasta sauces.

Broccoli Dip

Serve with raw vegetable sticks or corn chips.

2   cups raw broccoli, cut into 1-inch pieces or small florets
2   tablespoons low-fat sour cream or nonfat plain yogurt
2   tablespoons low-fat mayonnaise
2   tablespoons finely chopped red onion
1   tablespoon finely chopped fresh or pickled jalapeño peppers (or to taste)
2   tablespoons chopped fresh herbs— cilantro, cinnamon basil, or lemon basil
     Salt to taste

Steam the broccoli for 12 minutes, or until tender, in ¼ cup water in a covered dish in the microwave, or in a covered 2-quart saucepan in 1 inch of boiling water. Drain into a colander and chill quickly under cold water. Place broccoli in a food processor or blender with the sour cream and mayonnaise. Puree until smooth and scrape into a small bowl. Stir in the onion, jalapeño, and cilantro. Add salt to taste.

Note: The broccoli needs to be cooked until it purees to a smooth consistency.

Preparation time: 20 minutes
Yield: 1½ cups

Broccoli and Cheese Loaf

This is a lovely souffléed vegetarian loaf. For a change, try substituting 1 pound of carrots, kale, or winter squash.

1   pound broccoli florets
1   tablespoon olive oil
1   leek, finely sliced (about 1 cup)
2   large cloves garlic, crushed
¼   cup chopped fresh parsley
¼   cup chopped fresh oregano or 1 tablespoon dried
8   ounces low-fat cottage cheese
2   large eggs, separated
¼   cup grated Parmesan cheese
¼   cup sharp cheddar cheese
1   teaspoon dry mustard
⅛   teaspoon cayenne pepper
1½   cups fresh whole wheat bread crumbs (3 medium-size bread slices)

Lightly oil a 9 × 5-inch loaf pan. Line with cooking paper and lightly oil. Steam broccoli in a covered 2-quart saucepan with 1 inch of water, or microwave in a 2-quart dish with ¼ cup water for 8 minutes, until tender. Drain and reserve. Heat the olive oil in a skillet over medium heat, add the leek, garlic, parsley, and oregano, and sauté 3 minutes. Spoon into a food processor or blender and puree with the cooked

broccoli, cottage cheese, and egg yolks. Using a rubber spatula, scrape into a large mixing bowl and stir in the bread crumbs and Parmesan and cheddar cheeses.

Place the egg whites in a large metal or glass bowl with the dry mustard and cayenne pepper. Beat until stiff peaks form, then fold into the broccoli mixture, one third at a time. Spoon into the prepared loaf pan and bake in a preheated 375° F oven for 30 minutes. Allow to cool in the pan 10 minutes. Turn out onto a serving plate and remove the cooking paper from the bottom. Cut into slices and serve with Fresh Tomato Sauce (see page 112) or Mushroom Sauce (see page 111).

Preparation time: 25 minutes
Cooking time: 30 minutes
Yield: 4 entree servings; 8 side-dish servings

In addition to tasting great on raw vegetables, Broccoli Dip makes a great topping for baked potatoes or pasta.

Cauliflower Blue Cheese Gratin

Crunchy and flavorful when raw, cauliflower turns sweet and nutty when cooked slightly. However, its basically bland flavor makes it ideal for teaming with strong cheeses and aromatic spices.

1	head cauliflower, separated into florets
1½	tablespoons olive oil
6	shallots, chopped (about ¾ cup)
2	tablespoons all-purpose flour
1½	cups skim or low-fat milk
	Salt and pepper to taste
¼	teaspoon ground nutmeg
¼	cup fresh parsley, chopped
4	ounces crumbled blue cheese
1	cup dry bread crumbs
	Freshly ground pepper

Steam the cauliflower florets for 10 minutes, until tender, in 1 inch of boiling water in a covered 2-quart saucepan. Or microwave for 10 minutes in ¼ cup of water in a covered 2-quart dish. Drain and transfer to a baking dish. Heat the oil in a small saucepan over medium heat, stir in the chopped shallots, and sauté for 2 minutes. Stir in the flour and cook for 1 minute. Stirring constantly, add the milk and cook until it thickens. Season with salt, pepper, nutmeg, and parsley. Pour the sauce over the cauliflower florets. Combine the crumbled blue cheese and bread crumbs and sprinkle over the top of the sauced cauliflower. Give a few twists of the pepper mill over the topping. Place the dish 6 inches under a preheated broiler and cook for 4 minutes, until the cheese is lightly toasted and melting. Serve immediately.

Note: Turn this recipe into a main-meal dish by adding 1 cup chopped walnuts to the blue cheese and bread crumb topping.

Preparation time: 15 minutes
Cooking time: 15 minutes
Yield: 4 servings

Curried Cauliflower Soup

1	2-pound cauliflower, separated into florets (about 6 cups)
3	tablespoons olive oil
1	large sweet onion, finely chopped (about 1¼ cups)
1	large red bell pepper, finely chopped (about 1 cup)
2	large ribs celery, finely chopped (about 1 cup)
4	cloves garlic, finely minced
2	tablespoons all-purpose flour
3	tablespoons mild curry powder
2	teaspoons ground coriander
2	teaspoons turmeric powder
1	teaspoon ground cumin
2	cups skim or low-fat milk
1½	cups vegetable stock (reconstituted from a bouillon cube), including the cauliflower liquid
1	cup nonfat, plain yogurt or low-fat sour cream
¼	cup chopped fresh parsley

Steam the cauliflower florets in ½ cup water in a covered dish in the microwave (or on top of the stove in a covered pan in 1 inch of water) for 12 to 15 minutes, until tender. Heat the oil in a 4-quart saucepan over medium heat, add the chopped onion, bell pepper, celery, and garlic. Sauté for 10 minutes, stirring occasionally. Combine the flour, curry powder, coriander, turmeric, and cumin. Stir into the onion mixture and cook 5 minutes. Pour in the vegetable stock and milk and cook for 8 to 10 minutes, stirring frequently, until the liquid thickens. Stir the cauliflower florets into the pan and continuing cooking for 5 minutes, until heated through. Remove from the heat. Stir a little of the hot soup into the yogurt and spoon this mixture back into the simmering liquid in the pan. Stir to combine. Serve immediately garnished with chopped parsley.

Preparation time: 15 minutes
Cooking time: 40 minutes
Yield: 4 to 6 servings

Curried Cauliflower Soup is both rich and pungent, and good for you, too.

BRUSSELS SPROUTS
BRASSICA OLERACEA VAR. GEMMIFERA

As many as 60 tiny heads sprout on 2-foot-high stalks. While the stalks are too tough to be edible, the tight-headed miniature cabbages are very crisp and tender when harvested as firm buds of 1 to 2 inches wide. Although commercial growers plant those varieties which produce medium to dark green sprouts, ruby red ones are available.

With all the improved varieties and the recommended shorter cooking times, brussels sprouts don't deserve such bad press. These little greens are delicious enough when young to eat raw, shredded in salads. The only bitter sprouts are old sprouts.

NUTRITIONAL VALUE
A half-cup, cooked, provides 561 IU vitamin A, 48.4 mg vitamin C, 247 mg potassium, and 28 mg calcium.

BUYING AND STORING
Green or red, the sweetest-tasting sprouts are those that have been touched with frost. Choose those with tightly furled leaves. They are sweeter than loose-headed sprouts. Loose and yellowing leaves guarantee bitter or flavorless sprouts.

Available commercially from October through March, brussels sprouts can be left on the stalks and wintered over in the ground. Refrigerate purchased sprouts in a perforated plastic bag for up to 5 days.

Made from low-fat milk, this Creamed Green Soup is rich in flavor only.

PREPARATION
Remove the outer leaves if damaged, trim the stem end, and cut a shallow cross on the bottom. When steamed for about 8 minutes, they retain their color and crisp texture. While still warm, toss in a mustard, curry, or shallot vinaigrette. Serve at room temperature with a sprinkling of Parmesan cheese and black pepper. Sprouts can also be steamed for 6 minutes, rolled in egg and in seasoned cornmeal or bread crumbs, and sautéed until golden.

Young, fresh sprouts can be frozen. Prepare as for steaming and blanch in boiling water for 2 minutes, plunge into iced water, drain, and pack into airtight containers.

Brussels sprouts, while small in size, are nutritional giants.

Creamed Green Soup

Make this soup with brussels sprouts or broccoli.

1	*tablespoon olive oil*
1	*medium-size, strong onion, chopped (about ¾ cup)*
¼	*cup chopped celery leaves or* **1** *tablespoon chopped fresh lovage*
6	*cups brussels sprouts, sliced in half or broccoli, cut in 1-inch pieces*
2	*cups vegetable stock*
1½	*cups low-fat milk*
¼	*teaspoon ground mace*
1	*tablespoon chopped fresh dill or* **1** *teaspoon dried* *Salt and pepper to taste*
½	*teaspoon sugar* *Cream or milk to thin*
¼	*cup chopped chives*

Heat the oil in a 4-quart saucepan and sauté the onion and celery leaves for 5 minutes over medium heat. Add the brussels sprouts to the pan with the stock and milk. Cover and bring to a boil over high heat. Reduce the heat and simmer for 15 minutes. Place one third of the soup at a time in a food processor, blender, or food mill. Puree the mixture. Return the soup to the pot and stir in the mace, dill, salt, pepper, and sugar. Add enough cream to thin mixture to a moderately thick, souplike texture. Heat through for 5 minutes. Ladle into soup bowls and garnish with chopped chives.

Preparation time: 15 minutes
Cooking time: 25 minutes
Yield: 4 servings

CABBAGES
BRASSICA OLERACEA VAR. CAPITATA

Green Cabbage

There are several varieties of large, ball-headed cabbages. Those that mature during July through October have compact heads varying in color from medium to dark green. The firm, large round or drum heads of the winter varieties range in color from blue-green to red-tinged-green to white. (White is an exceptionally good storer and is preferred for making cole slaw and sauerkraut.) Winter cabbages are harvested November through March.

NUTRITIONAL VALUE
A half-cup, cooked and shredded, provides 64 IU vitamin A, 18 mg vitamin C, 25 mg calcium, and 154 mg potassium.

Red Cabbage

A smaller, ball-headed summer cabbage with burgundy-red leaves. This is harvested around September for immediate eating or left in the ground until November and stored for winter use. A favorite for adding color to cole slaw, for pickling, or for sweet-and-sour dishes.

NUTRITIONAL VALUE
A half-cup, cooked and shredded, provides 20 IU vitamin A, 25.8 mg vitamin C, 105 mg potassium, and 28 mg calcium.

Savoy Cabbage

A dark green cabbage with a tight and curly head, with crinkly leaves. These have ball or drum heads and are grown for harvesting September through March. Depending on variety, the heads range in size from medium to large. Savoy is the one to choose when stuffing a whole cabbage—the leaves hold their shape better than other cabbages.

NUTRITIONAL VALUE
A half-cup, cooked and shredded, provides 649 IU vitamin A, 12.4 mg vitamin C, 134 mg potassium, and 22 mg calcium.

Spring Cabbage

This dark green variety is cultivated as a nonheading cabbage. The leaves are harvested in the spring before the head forms and are sold as spring greens or collards. If heads are allowed to form, most are conical and solid. Harvested March through May.

NUTRITIONAL VALUE
A half-cup, cooked and chopped, provides 2,109 IU vitamin A, 9.3 mg vitamin C, 74 mg calcium, and 88 mg potassium.

CHINESE CABBAGE

Although members of the *Brassica* group, Chinese cabbages are not considered true cabbages.

Bok Choy
Brassica chinensis

Also called "pak choi," this is a nonheading cabbage. The leaves are dark green with broad, white, fleshy stems that resemble chard more than regular cabbage. Excellent for slicing and stir-frying or braising in a little rice wine and soy sauce.

NUTRITIONAL VALUE
A half-cup, cooked and shredded, provides 2,183 IU vitamin A, 22 mg vitamin C, 315 mg potassium, and 79 mg calcium.

The tender, fleshy leaves of bok choy can liven up any meal.

Celery Cabbage
Brassica pekinensis

Also called Napa, Nappa, and Chinese cabbage. There are short- and long-heading types, the most familiar of which are the long *michihli* and *pe-tsai* varieties. The white stalks are quite broad (although not as broad as bok choy) and support pale- to mid-green leaves that may be crinkly or relatively smooth. They are mildly sweet and crunchy with some varieties possessing a delicate celery flavor. Very good for eating raw in salads, sautéeing with onions for a side dish, or stir-frying with mixed vegetables.

NUTRITIONAL VALUE
A half-cup, cooked and shredded, provides 575 IU vitamin A, 9 mg vitamin C, 134 mg potassium, 57 mcg folacin, and 19 mg calcium.

KALE AND COLLARD
BRASSICA OLERACEA VAR. ACEPHALA

Kale, borecole, and collard are types of nonheading cabbage. Different varieties produce leaves that are ruffled, curly, or flat (like collard) and colors that vary from dark green to bluish green. The tender young leaves of kale are the mildest. These are cool-weather greens, and when grown during the warmer weather, the large, mature leaves develop a bitter flavor.

Several varieties of kale have the name "Scotch" (as in "Blue Scotch") and there is, in fact, a type of Scotch kale (*Brassica napus*) that is in the same group as rutabagas. The name "kale"

evolved from the Scottish word for cabbage.

Add young kale and collard greens to a salad. They can be shredded and steamed in an inch of water for 10 minutes or stir-fried like spinach. Mature leaves belong in the soup pot or a casserole.

NUTRITIONAL VALUE
A half-cup, cooked and chopped, provides 4,810 IU vitamin A, 26.7 mg vitamin C, 148 mg potassium, and 47 mg calcium.

BUYING AND STORING CABBAGES AND LEAFY GREENS
Look for crisp, green leaves and firm heads. Avoid limp, yellowing leaves, which may be a sign of poor storage, old produce, or overly matured vegetables—these vegetables have been robbed of some of their desirable nutritional qualities.

Store greens in plastic bags in the refrigerator for 2 to 3 days. Whole cabbages will keep for 1 week or longer.

PREPARATION OF CABBAGES AND LEAFY GREENS
Remove the outer wilted or discolored leaves and save for the compost heap. Cut cabbages in half or quarters and cut out the lowest part of the hard stem. Depending on the recipe, cut into smaller wedges or shred.

Steam sections in an inch of water for 15 minutes, shredded cabbage for just 8 to 10 minutes. Cook 4 wedges or 4 cups shredded for the same length of time in the microwave with ¼ cup of water.

Chinese Celery Cabbage Stir-Fry

2	*tablespoons vegetable oil*
2	*pounds cabbage cut in 2-inch pieces (about 8 cups)*
¾	*cup water*
¼	*cup rice vinegar*
2	*tablespoons soy sauce*
1½	*tablespoons cornstarch*
1	*tablespoon grated fresh ginger*
1	*3-inch hot chile (to taste), stem removed and thinly sliced on the diagonal with seeds intact*

Heat the oil in a wok over medium-high heat. Add the cabbage and cook 3 minutes, stirring frequently. Remove from the wok to a dish. Combine the water, rice vinegar, soy sauce, cornstarch, and grated ginger. Pour into the wok and stir constantly until it thickens, in about 1 minute. Return cabbage to the wok, add the sliced hot chiles, and stir-fry for 1 minute. Serve immediately.

Note: Substitute bok choy or chard, if desired. Choose 1 (or more to taste) long hot cayenne, or 2 of the smaller hot serrano or Thai chiles.

Preparation time: 10 minutes
Cooking time: 7 minutes
Yield: 4 to 6 servings

Sweet and Sour Cole Slaw

This makes a tasty, refreshing change from creamy mayonnaise cole slaw.

½   pound light green cabbage, shredded (about 2 cups)
½   pound red cabbage, shredded (about 2 cups)
2   large carrots, peeled and shredded (about 2 cups)
1   medium red onion, cut in half and thinly sliced (about 1 cup)
½   cup vegetable oil
¼   cup cider vinegar
¼   cup water
1   tablespoon superfine sugar
     Salt and pepper to taste
2   to 4 cloves garlic, crushed
1   tablespoon celery seeds
¼   cup chopped fresh dill or 1 tablespoon dried

In a large bowl, combine all the vegetables. Mix the rest of the ingredients in a screw-top jar and shake together. Pour over the slaw and toss to distribute the dressing. Refrigerate for several hours to blend the flavors.

Preparation time: 15 minutes
Yield: 4 to 6 servings

Salmon-Stuffed Cabbage Sandwich

Use fresh poached or canned salmon, or substitute canned tuna for a change. Serve with a knife and fork.

2   cups fresh poached salmon or canned salmon, drained
3   tablespoons low-fat mayonnaise or sour cream
1   teaspoon prepared mustard
1   to 2 teaspoons chopped fresh tarragon (to taste) or 2 tablespoons chopped fresh chives
     Salt and pepper to taste
½   small cucumber, peeled, seeds removed, and diced small (about ½ cup)
8   small (sandwich-bread size) cabbage leaves—red, savoy, or Chinese nappa
1   cup bean sprouts

Place the salmon in a medium mixing bowl. Remove any skin, bone, or cartilage and flake the flesh. Add the mayonnaise, mustard, tarragon, salt, and pepper and stir to combine. Stir in the chopped cucumber. Arrange 4 cabbage leaves on individual plates. Spoon a quarter of the salmon mixture onto each leaf, sprinkle with 2 tablespoons of bean sprouts, and top with a cabbage leaf. Refrigerate until ready to serve.

Preparation time: 20 minutes
Yield: 4 sandwiches

Colorful and tasty, Sweet and Sour Cole Slaw is the perfect dish to serve on a hot summer day.

KOHLRABI

BRASSICA OLERACEA
CAULORAPA VAR.
GONGYLOIDES

This is a cabbage turnip. The bulb, or globe, varies in color from green to cream to pale purple; it is, quite simply, the swollen base of the stem. It is sweet and crunchy when young, with a flavor not unlike turnip. The young leaves are slightly spicy and taste similar to mustard or turnip greens. They can be added to a salad or a soup, or steamed like spinach.

NUTRITIONAL VALUE
The swollen kohlrabi globe has a higher nutritional value than turnip root. A half-cup, cooked, provides 29 IU vitamin A, 44.3 mg vitamin C, 279 mg potassium, and 20 mg calcium.

BUYING AND STORING KOHLRABI
Kohlrabi can tolerate warmer weather than turnips and are available for a few months when turnips are not. Look for globes that are about the size of a large round apple, feel firm, and have bright green leaves attached. Remove the few sprigs of greens (add to the compost or the soup pot), and store the globe in a perforated plastic bag in the refrigerator for no more than a week.

PREPARATION OF KOHLRABI
The thick skin on the bulb needs to be peeled. Young, crisp kohlrabi is good for grating and tossing with salad greens or for slicing thinly to accompany a dip. Substitute larger bulbs for turnips or rutabagas in soups, gratins, stir-fries, and casseroles.

Don't pass up sweet, crunchy, and extremely versatile kohlrabi.

Kale and Kohlrabi Soup

This is a good winter peasant soup that can be made just as easily with collards or spring cabbage and turnip. The barley has a slightly nutty texture, and the vegetables are brightly colored.

Although Kale and Kohlrabi Soup has its roots in Scotland, it resembles many soups from around the globe.

8	cups water
2	large carrots, peeled and chopped (about 2 cups)
1	small kohlrabi, peeled and diced (about 1 cup)
1	large, strong onion, chopped (about 1¼ cups)
1	leek, trimmed, cleaned, and thinly sliced (about 2 cups)
1	rib celery with leaves, chopped (about ½ cup)
½	cup uncooked pearl barley Salt and pepper to taste
1	pound kale, stems discarded, and roughly chopped
2	teaspoons dried thyme leaves

Bring the water to a boil over high heat in a heavy 5-quart pan. Add all of the ingredients except the kale and thyme, lower the heat, and simmer for 45 minutes. Add the kale and thyme and simmer for 15 minutes longer. Accompany with a generous serving of garlic bread.

Note: For a softer barley, precook 15 minutes before adding the chopped vegetables.

Preparation time: 20 minutes
Cooking time: 1 hour
Yield: 4 to 6 servings

CARROTS

DAUCUS CAROTA, FAMILY UMBELLIFERAE

Native to Europe and Asia, carrots have been cultivated for over 2,000 years from a variety of the wild Queen-Anne's-lace. By the sixteenth century, they were an important source of food in Europe, with the Dutch and the British eating more carrots than anyone else. They became a major world crop during the early 1900s. Today there are many varieties, in all shapes and sizes. Some of the short varieties are as round and small as golf balls or short and blunt like fingers. Intermediates tend to be thick and stumpy, uniformly cylindrical, or broad and tapered. Finally, there are the long, tapered giants. Carrot colors range from yellow-orange to deep orange. The crunchy, juicy texture and the sweet flavor rival those of an apple.

NUTRITIONAL VALUE

Carrots are loaded with carotene (pro-vitamin A), which promotes good night vision and reduces the risk of many forms of cancer. Munching on a single large carrot (¾ cup shredded) provides 20,000 IU of vitamin A. Carrots contain moderate amounts of calcium, magnesium, phosphorus, vitamin C, and folacin, and a good dose of potassium. When cooked, they lose most of their vitamin C content.

BUYING AND STORING

Young, tender, summer-fresh carrots are the sweetest. Store carrots in plastic bags in the vegetable drawer of the refrigerator for 2 weeks. They will keep longer but sprout fine root hairs and lose their sweet flavor. For longer storage, freeze baby carrots whole and cut the larger varieties into sticks or thin slices and freeze in airtight containers. The home gardener can store them in sand or plastic containers (with a few air holes) in a root cellar where the air is moist and cool.

Carrots are available commercially canned, frozen, and as a very nutritious juice.

PREPARATION

Very fresh, tender carrots need only rinsing and scrubbing. Julienne and sauté in a little oil or butter, or steam in the microwave until just cooked through. They can also be popped into the lunch box for a raw, sweet treat.

Slice, dice, and shred carrots raw in salads or serve them crunchy in stir-fries. They add sweetness and flavor to soups, stews, and casseroles. Carrots can be made into marmalades, pickles, baby food, and wine. They add moisture to cakes, muffins, and cookies.

Older carrots sometimes need the skin removed with a potato peeler or at least need to be scraped with a paring knife. These are good for shredding and baking, slicing into the soup pot, or boiling and combining with turnips, potatoes, or parsnips.

Raw or cooked, carrots are storehouses of natural beta carotene.

Carrot and Orange Soup

This soup is delicious hot or chilled. For a more intense orange flavor, add 1 teaspoon of grated orange rind.

2	tablespoons margarine or butter
8	large carrots, thinly sliced (about 4 cups)
1	large potato, cut in ½-inch cubes (about 1 cup)
1	large onion, quartered and thinly sliced (about 1 cup)
2	cloves garlic, finely minced
5	cups vegetable stock
	Salt and pepper to taste
1	cup orange juice
3	thin orange slices, cut in half and twisted, for garnish
12	mint leaves (orange mint if possible) for garnish

Melt the margarine in a heavy 4-quart saucepan over medium heat. Add the carrots, potato, onion, and garlic, and sauté for 5 minutes. Add the vegetable stock, salt, and pepper. Bring to a fast boil, reduce the heat, cover the pan, and simmer for 20 minutes, until the vegetables are tender.

Puree in a blender or food processor in 2 or 3 batches. Return to the pan, add the orange juice, and heat through or chill. Serve each soup dish garnished with a twisted orange half-slice and 2 orange mint leaves.

Preparation time: 15 minutes
Cooking time: 25 minutes
Yield: 6 servings

For a naturally sweeter filling, substitute chopped dates for the apricots in Apricot-Ricotta Carrot Roll.

Apricot-Ricotta Carrot Roll

Filled, rolled cakes always look special and are great for festive occasions. Despite their complicated appearance, they are easy to make.

4	large eggs, separated
¾	cup superfine sugar
1	large carrot, grated (about 1 cup)
½	cup all-purpose flour
1	teaspoon ground cinnamon
½	teaspoon ground nutmeg
1	teaspoon ground allspice
	Confectioners' icing sugar

Apricot Filling

1	cup dried apricot halves, chopped
½	cup orange juice or brandy, heated
1½	cups ricotta cheese
½	cup confectioners' icing sugar (to taste)
1	teaspoon ground cinnamon
3	tablespoons blanched almonds, chopped
1	tablespoon blanched almond halves, toasted

Preheat the oven to 375° F and lightly oil a 15½- × 10½-inch jelly-roll pan. Line with waxed baking paper; lightly oil and flour. In a mixing bowl, beat egg yolks and ½ cup of sugar for 3 to 4 minutes until creamy. Stir in the carrot. In a separate bowl, sift together the flour, cinnamon, nutmeg, and allspice and gently stir into the egg yolk mixture. In a large metal or glass mixing bowl, beat the egg whites until thickened. Gradually beat in the remaining ¼ cup sugar until thick and glossy but not dry. Stir ¼ of the beaten egg whites into the flour mixture to lighten it. Gradually fold in the remaining egg whites until no white streaks remain.

Spoon the batter into the prepared pan and well into the corners. With a very light touch, spread evenly to smooth. Place in the middle of the oven and bake for 15 minutes, until firm and slightly springy to the touch in the center. To unmold, loosen the sides of the cake with a knife and invert onto a sheet of waxed baking paper sprinkled with confectioners' sugar. Carefully peel off the waxed paper that was in the pan and roll up from a short end with the new waxed paper inside. Place seamside down on a wire tray and allow to cool.

Note: To freeze the cake at this point, wrap the roll in heavy-duty aluminum foil to exclude all air. Thaw before unrolling and filling.

To Make Filling
Place the chopped apricots in a small bowl and cover with the hot orange juice. Cover and allow to absorb the juice for 15 minutes. Drain and reserve the remaining juice. Place ricotta, confectioner's icing sugar, and cinnamon in a food processor or blender and puree until smooth. Turn into a bowl and add the apricot pieces and the chopped almonds. Add the remaining juice for a softer filling. Unroll the cake, remove the waxed baking paper, and spread with the filling to within a half-inch of the edges. Reroll the cake, place seamside down on a cake plate, sprinkle with confectioner's icing sugar, and decorate with toasted almond halves. Refrigerate until ready to serve.

Preparation time: 30 minutes
Cooking time: 15 minutes
Yield: 8 to 12 servings

Growing throughout Europe and in regions of northern Africa, wild celery was harvested from its marshy environs by the Egyptians, Greeks, and Romans. Until well into the Middle Ages, "smallage" was used exclusively for its medicinal properties. During the sixteenth century, the French and the Italians finally decided that smallage was a tasty addition to the soup pot. By 1874, celery was being grown in North America, in Kalamazoo, Michigan, as a commercial crop, and marketed to passengers who traveled on the Michigan Central Railroad. From such a modest beginning, it is now one of the major salad crops in the United States.

Of the many varieties of celery, a few are trenched (mounded with soil) and develop white, tender stems. When left untrenched, they grow crisp, light green or yellow-green stems. Several other varieties are self-blanching and produce naturally creamy white and solid white stems. Celery earned its name *graveolens*, which means "strong smelling," from its original, bitter flavor and strong odor. With the new cultivars, the name hardly applies today.

CELERIAC

APIUM GRAVEOLENS VAR. RAPACEUM

This is a large, knobby root and tastes like stalk celery. Also called celery root and celery-turnip root, its thick skin needs peeling before it is cooked for 15 minutes or shredded and added to salads like *celeri-rave remoulade*. Like potatoes, it can be made into pancakes, purees, soups, and gratins.

NUTRITIONAL VALUE
Green celery offers little in the way of vitamins A and C or calcium, but contains more than the white varieties.

Celeriac is high in calcium, phosphorous, and potassium.

Celery leaves can be used as an herb in salads, rice dishes, spaghetti sauces, and soups.

BUYING AND STORING

Select heads of celery with firm, unblemished stalks and fresh, bright yellow or green leaves. Store for up to 2 weeks in a plastic bag in the vegetable drawer of the refrigerator. The home gardener can keep celery for as long as 4 months in a root cellar with the temperature just above freezing, high humidity, and little air circulation; pull the celery from the garden, plant roots up to crown in a tray of soil, and keep moist all winter. Avoid splashing the stalks and leaves. Commercial celery is available year-round.

PREPARATION

Tender young celery stalks are sweet and mild, delicious for munching with dips or for stuffing with a flavored cheese. Finely chopped, they make a welcome addition to salad dishes. Crisp outer stalks are perfect for slicing thin and tossing into a stir-fry. Chopped celery is a tasty flavor in stuffings, spaghetti sauces, stews, and soups. Homemade cream of celery soup is one of the easiest and most flavorful in a cook's repertoire. Large pieces of stems can be cooked au gratin or served in a creamy cheese sauce.

Pureed Celery Root and Potatoes

Celery root gives a delectable flavor to boiling potatoes.

1	*pound celery root, peeled, sliced ½ inch thick, and dropped in water containing 2 tablespoons lemon juice*
1	*pound boiling potatoes, peeled and sliced ½ inch thick*
1	*leek, white part only, cleaned and sliced ½ inch thick*
3	*tablespoons margarine or butter*
3	*tablespoons low-fat sour cream*
	Salt and pepper to taste
¼	*cup chopped fresh parsley*

Drain the celery root, place in a 3-quart pot with the potatoes and leek, and cover with water. Put the lid on the pot and bring the water to a boil over high heat. Reduce the heat to low and simmer for 25 to 30 minutes, until the celery root and potatoes are very tender. Drain and reserve the tasty water for cooking another day. Puree in 2 batches in the food processor until smooth. Return to the pot and combine with the margarine, sour cream, salt, pepper, and parsley. Spoon into a serving dish and serve immediately or cover and keep warm in a very low oven.

Preparation time: 15 minutes
Cooking time: 30 minutes
Yield: 4 to 6 servings

Celery and Stilton Soup

This classic English soup is full of flavor and hearty enough for a main meal. Serve it with a mixed green salad and easy homemade bread sticks.

2	*tablespoons margarine or butter*
2	*medium-size onions, finely chopped (about 1½ cups)*
4	*ribs celery, finely chopped (about 2 cups)*
3	*tablespoons all-purpose flour*
4	*cups skim milk*
8	*ounces Stilton cheese, crumbled*
½	*teaspoon white pepper*
¼	*cup half-and-half*

Melt margarine in a heavy 3- to 4-quart saucepan over medium heat. Add onions and celery, and sauté for 7 minutes. Stir in the flour and cook 2 minutes. Stir in the milk and continue stirring until the sauce thickens. Reduce heat and simmer, stirring occasionally, for 10 minutes, until the vegetables are tender. Reserve 2 tablespoons of the Stilton for garnish and add the rest to the pan with the pepper. Stir until the soup is smooth. Stir in the half-and-half. Serve in warm soup bowls and garnish with the reserved Stilton.

Preparation time: 15 minutes
Cooking time: 30 minutes
Yield: 4 to 6 servings

Bread Sticks

8   ounces (2 sticks) margarine or butter
½   to 1 cup parsley
1   French baguette, cut in half
     lengthwise
     Freshly ground pepper
½   cup sesame seeds

Process the margarine and the parsley until smooth. Spread onto the bread and season with several grinds of the pepper mill. Sprinkle each half with sesame seeds and cut into 1-inch slices. Bake in a 250° F oven for 15 minutes, until lightly browned and crunchy.

Preparation time: 10 minutes
Cooking time: 15 minutes
Yield: 4 to 6 servings

Make Celery and Sweet Pepper Salad the main course by tossing the dressed vegetables with cooked cubed potatoes, pasta spirals, or couscous.

Celery Root (Celeriac) Remoulade

2   pounds celery root
2   tablespoons white vinegar
½   cup mayonnaise
1   tablespoon prepared mild mustard
1   tablespoon lemon juice
1   tablespoon fresh chopped parsley
1   tablespoon chopped chives
1   teaspoon chopped fresh tarragon
1   teaspoon chopped capers
1   tablespoon chopped dill pickles

1. Peel the celery root, cut into thin strips, and drop the strips into a bowl of water containing the vinegar.
2. Combine the rest of the ingredients in a medium-size serving bowl.
3. Drain the celery root, blot dry between paper towels, and stir into the mayonnaise mixture. Cover and refrigerate several hours.

Note: Cut celery root discolors quickly, so dip it in acidulated water right after peeling and cutting. Or blanch the shredded or julienned strands in boiling water for 30 seconds and then refresh in a colander under cold running water.

Preparation time: 30 minutes
Yield: 4 servings

Celery and Sweet Pepper Salad

4   small ribs celery, trimmed and sliced
     diagonally in ½-inch pieces
2   sweet peppers, seeds and membranes
     removed, and cut in 1- × ½-inch
     pieces
½   small cucumber, peeled and chopped
2   scallions, thinly sliced
1   inch of fresh ginger root, grated
2   cloves garlic, crushed
2   tablespoons vegetable oil
2   tablespoons soy sauce
1   tablespoon lime juice
2   tablespoons white wine vinegar
1   teaspoon brown sugar
1   teaspoon dry mustard
½   teaspoon hot chile flakes or hot
     paprika powder
     Ginger root slivers
     Celery leaves
¼   cup toasted sesame seeds

Combine the celery, peppers, cucumber, scallions, and ginger in a large mixing bowl. Mix together the garlic, oil, soy sauce, lime juice, vinegar, brown sugar, mustard, and chile flakes. Pour over the vegetables, toss to coat, and refrigerate for several hours for the flavors to blend. Divide between 4 salad plates and garnish with ginger, celery leaves, and toasted sesame seeds.

Note: For a more colorful dish, use yellow, orange, or red bell peppers. For a change of pace, stir-fry the vegetables for 3 minutes, toss with the dressing, and serve immediately.

Preparation time: 15 minutes
Yield: 4 servings

CORN

ZEA MAYS

Cultivated for about 4,000 years, corn is native to Central and Andean South America. A staple food of the Incas, Mayas, and Aztecs, it was transported into North America by migrating Indians and took centuries to reach the eastern United States. The Spanish conquistadors took this *mahiz* to Europe during the fifteenth century and one hundred years later, aided by the Portuguese, "maize" spread to Africa, Asia, East India, and the rest of the world. In the New World, early settlers owed their very existence to Indian corn and by the late nineteenth century, the corn industry played a major role in America's economy.

Although there are four major types of corn (flint [Indian], dent [field], popcorn, and sweet), hybridized corn is the sweetest. "Super sweet," "ultra sweet," and "extra sweet," were the early hybrids in the 1950s. Then came "sugary enhanced" in the 1960s. This corn is not sweeter, but it retains the sweet flavor for a longer time both on and off the stalk. Where regular sweet corn has

sugar levels from 5 to 10 percent, the sugary enhanced type contains 15 to 18 percent, and a super sweet (also ultra and extra) has 25 to 30 percent. Today, hybrid varieties number in the thousands. Early in the season, corn is available at the local farmstand.

NUTRITIONAL VALUE

High in protein (3 grams in an ear of white or yellow), corn was well named when the native Indians called it *maize*, meaning "our life." Swedish botanist Linnaeus echoed this sentiment when, in 1737, he gave it the Latin name *zea mays*, meaning "that which sustains the Mayas." A major source of complex carbohydrates, sweet corn offers modest amounts of calcium, magnesium, phosphorous, and vitamin C. White and yellow corn ears are a good source of potassium, but only yellow contains more than a trace of vitamin A.

BUYING AND STORING

Most sweet corn does not transport well, and the crunchiest and sweetest

corn is that bought from local farmers the same day it is picked. An old favorite, because it has a true sweet "corn" flavor, is yellow Golden Bantam, but like the white favorite, Silver Queen, and the yellow-and-white kernels of Butter and Sugar, it doesn't hold up to transportation. Without doubt, these standard varieties are best eaten within hours or, at least, the same day they are picked. Newer varieties like Extra Early Sweet, How Sweet It Is, Illini Chief Extra-Sweet, Butterfruit, and Double Delight stay sweeter for a longer period. However, many people feel that the sweetness of "extra sweets" interferes with the true corn flavor.

Depending on the region, the first harvest of local corn can be expected in early July. With the usual successive plantings, harvesting may continue into October. Contingent on variety, corn plants grow from 6 to 10 feet tall and produce from one to three ears of corn ranging in size from 7 to 10 inches long.

Choose ears of corn encased in smooth, bright green husks and refrige-

Corn, sunkissed, sweet, and succulent, is the essence of summer.

rate immediately. Do not remove the husks until ready to use, otherwise the kernels will dry out. Corn on the cob is best prepared the day it's picked—once harvested, the sugars turn to starch very quickly and not only is the sweetness lost, but the texture changes from crunchy to soft and chewy. If it's not to be eaten soon after picking or buying, refrigerate in plastic bags for up to two days and then use in combination dishes.

PREPARATION
Shuck the corn just before cooking. To do this, pull back the green husk leaves and snap off at the bottom. Remove the silks by twisting the ear between damp hands or take a damp kitchen towel and rub the silks off very gently.

To prepare whole ears of corn: bring a large pot of water to a boil, drop in the ears, and heat through for 2 to 4 minutes. At 2 minutes, the raw flavor is removed, the ears are hot, and the kernels still crunchy. A cooking time longer than 5 minutes makes them soft and starchy—an undesirable texture when eating on the cob. Roll in melted butter and eat. Whole ears can be barbecued in their husks or shucked and wrapped in foil.

To freeze whole ears of corn, blanch for 2 to 4 minutes and drop immediately into a bowl of iced water kept chilled under a faucet of running cold water. Drain, blot dry, pack in plastic bags (squeeze out *all* the air), and freeze.

To remove the kernels, shuck and remove the silks from the ear. Place the corn upright in a bowl or on a plate and scrape off the kernels with a sharp paring knife, working from the top down to the bottom of the ears. When sautéeing, add fresh kernels 1 to 2 minutes before the end of cooking time and frozen kernels 3 to 5 minutes before. Use kernels for making spoon bread, fritters, custard pudding, succotash, creamed corn, muffins, or corn oysters.

Corn and Leek Quiche

This quiche is quite delicious for brunch or dinner. Serve with a large mixed green salad and sliced tomatoes.

1   single 9-inch pie crust
1   tablespoon olive oil
1   leek, trimmed, washed, and thinly sliced (about 1 cup)
1   medium red bell pepper, diced small
2   large eggs
1   cup skim or low-fat milk
¾   cup low-fat, creamed cottage cheese
    Salt and pepper to taste
1½ cups corn kernels, fresh, canned, or frozen (thawed and drained)
½   cup grated reduced-fat cheddar cheese
½   cup chopped fresh basil

Preheat the oven to 425° F and lightly oil a 9-inch pie dish.

Roll out the pastry into ⅛-inch-thick circle large enough to overhang the pie dish by at least ½ inch. Fit into the pie dish and turn the excess pastry under. Pinch down and flute. Refrigerate.

Heat the oil in a skillet over medium heat and sauté the leeks and sweet pepper for 3 minutes. Remove from the heat. Beat together the eggs, milk, cottage cheese, salt, and pepper in a medium-size mixing bowl. Stir in the corn kernels, cheddar cheese, and chopped basil. Spoon the leek and pepper mixture into the chilled pie shell and pour the egg mixture over the top.

Place in the middle of the oven and bake 10 minutes at 425° F. Reduce the heat to 350° F and bake for 30 to 35 minutes longer, until a knife inserted in the center comes out clean. Remove from the oven and cool 10 to 15 minutes on a wire rack before cutting. Serve warm or at room temperature.

Preparation time: 15 minutes
Cooking time: 45 minutes
Yield: 6 servings

Double Corn Muffins

Serve up these savory muffins as a lunch or dinner bread.

1   cup corn meal
1   cup all-purpose flour
1   tablespoon baking powder
½   teaspoon baking soda
1   tablespoon ground coriander
⅓   cup vegetable oil
2   large eggs
1   cup buttermilk
2   tablespoons chopped jalapeño peppers (fresh or pickled)
1½ cups corn kernels, fresh, canned, or frozen (thawed and drained)

Preheat the oven to 425° F and lightly oil a 12-cup muffin pan.

Mix the corn meal, flour, baking powder, baking soda, and coriander in a large bowl. Make a well in the center. In a medium bowl, beat together the oil, eggs, and buttermilk. Stir in the chopped jalapeños and corn kernels. Pour this mixture into the center of the dry ingredients and stir until just combined so that the mixture is lumpy. Fill the muffin cups with the mixture and place in the center of the oven. Bake 20 minutes, until a skewer inserted in the center comes out clean. Remove from the oven and leave in the pan 5 minutes. Remove from the cups and cool on a wire rack.

Note: Serve warm, or reheat wrapped in foil in the oven on low or wrapped in waxed paper in the microwave. If desired, when cool, place in a heavy plastic freezer bag and freeze for up to six months. For a sweeter breakfast version, increase the honey to ½ cup, add 1 cup chopped pecans and 2 teaspoons ground cinnamon (eliminate the jalapeños and ground coriander).

Preparation time: 10 minutes
Cooking time: 20 minutes
Yield: 12 muffins

Packed with nutrition, Double Corn Muffins are also colorful and delicious.

Dried beans, peas, and lentils are the seeds of pod-bearing plants called legumes. While some varieties have been cultivated for centuries in North and South America, others have been grown for thousands of years in China, India, Africa, and the Middle East. Although some are also eaten fresh—such as lima beans, black-eyed peas, fava beans, and flageolets—most are grown to be consumed in their dried form.

Azuki Beans
Phaseolus angularis
Native to China, azukis are small red or black beans that are particularly sweet and flavorful. They are commonly combined with rice and added to soups.

Black Beans
Phaseolus vulgaris
Also known as turtle beans, these are small, jet-black beans with a white interior. They are most often used in Latin-American and Mexican recipes and served with rice.

Beans are high in protein and come in many shapes and colors, making them very versatile

Garbanzo Beans
Cicer arietinum

Also called ceci beans and chick-peas, these Asian natives are available whole and split. Delicious in soups and pasta sauces, these firm, nutty-flavored beans are the main ingredients in hummus, which is a thick, garlicky dip, and falafel, a savory, fried vegetarian patty.

Great Northern Beans
Phaseolus vulgaris

Also called *haricot*, these are large, flat white beans that are used in soups, stews, casseroles, and other baked dishes.

Kidney Beans
Phaseolus vulgaris

Red kidney beans vary in shades from light to dark. Their firm texture and distinct flavor is suited to long cooking in casseroles and soups; they are most commonly used in chili recipes. White kidney beans are called cannellini and fagiola beans; they have a tender skin and soft texture. These are best used in quick-cooking pasta sauces or tossed with a salad dressing.

Lentils
Lens esculenta

Lentils are available in brown, green, red, or yellow, and in small or large varieties. Their main advantage is they can be cooked without any presoaking in as little as 15 to 20 minutes. Used in salads, soups, and Indian *dal* vegetable side dishes.

Navy Beans
Phaseolus vulgaris

A smaller variety of *haricot*, these are famous for their use in Boston baked beans and French *cassoulets*. They are the main beans used for canned baked beans.

Pinto Beans
Phaseolus vulgaris

Pintos are pale, pinkish beans with a strong flavor suitable for use in spicy, chili dishes.

Soybeans
Glycine max

Native to Asia, soybeans have been grown in the United States since the 1940s and are exported to Japan. They are made into flour, oil, milk, bean curd (tofu), fermented soy and shoyu sauces, miso pastes, and numerous plastic products. They are a major source of vegetable protein in a vegetarian diet. Black soybeans are made into fermented black bean sauce, which is used in many Chinese dishes.

Split Green Peas
Pisum sativum

Although they are made mostly into pea soup, split green peas are also made into a vegetable side dish in some European countries. In England, they were used to make pease pudding, and dried peas were frequently served in school lunch programs. While yellow split peas are not as popular, they are equally nourishing. Split peas do not need soaking.

Urd Beans
Phaseolus mungo

Native to India, these are small, dull black beans used in East Indian *dal* recipes. For this reason, they are often referred to as *urd dal* beans.

NUTRITIONAL VALUE

Leguminous plants that produce edible seeds are high in protein and fiber and low in fat. Soybeans are not as low in polyunsaturated fat as other varieties of beans, but they are higher in protein. Dried legumes are also high in minerals and vitamins and provide thiamine, niacin, vitamin B_6, and folacin. They are also a good source of calcium, phosphorus, iron, and potassium.

BUYING AND STORING

Canned beans are just as high in nutrients and fiber as dried beans, although some brands contain more salt than others.

Dried beans store for months when kept in a cool, dry place. Cooked beans can be refrigerated for one week or so. For longer storage of cooked beans, freeze for up to six months.

PREPARATION

Dried beans need presoaking. The traditional method is to soak in cold water to cover overnight or 6 to 8 hours. This is the preferred method because the beans absorb less water during cooking and they cook more uniformly. When beans are presoaked and the water discarded, it helps to eliminate the gas produced by the complex sugars. People who do not eat dried beans frequently suffer the most from irritation of the intestines, which causes flatulence. People who are particularly sensitive to intestinal irritation should soak the beans (use 6 to 8 cups of water per pound of beans), discard the water, cover with fresh water, and cook for 30 minutes. This water should then be discarded another one or two times, and fresh water added and cooking continued until the beans are tender. It is important to note that some water-soluble nutrients are lost when the water is changed several times.

The quick-soak method is to cover the beans with 6 cups of water, bring to a boil for 2 minutes, cover and remove from the heat. Allow to stand one hour. Drain, cover with fresh water, and simmer for the required length of time.

Pasta Salad with Cannellini Beans and Red Peppers

If you have a few cans of beans in the pantry, this dish can be made in 15 minutes. Substitute any kind of beans for the cannellini beans and add more chopped or shredded vegetables, as desired. You may want to throw in a few tablespoons of spicy taco sauce.

1	*pound elbow macaroni*
2	*16-ounce cans cannellini beans*
2	*medium red bell peppers, diced small (about 1½ cups)*
1	*medium red onion, thinly sliced*
1	*cup basil leaves, shredded, or parsley leaves, chopped*
4	*large garlic cloves, crushed*
1	*teaspoon crushed dried hot pepper flakes*
½	*cup vegetable oil*
½	*cup lemon juice (from 3 to 4 lemons)*
1	*tablespoon prepared mustard*
½	*pound cherry tomatoes, cut in half*

Cook the macaroni in 4 quarts boiling water for approximately 8 to 10 minutes, until a little more cooked than al dente. Drain and rinse under cold water. While the pasta is cooking, combine the beans (plus any liquid in the cans°), bell pepper, onion, and basil leaves in a large serving bowl. Combine the garlic, hot pepper flakes, oil, lemon juice, and mustard in a screw-top jar and shake to combine. Add the pasta to the beans and vegetables and mix in with the garlic dressing. Gently toss in the halved cherry tomatoes. Serve immediately or refrigerate.
°Anyone with high blood pressure or other sodium-related problems should discard the liquid.

Preparation time: 5 minutes
Cooking time: 15 minutes
Yield: 6 servings

Chick-Pea and Scallion Potato Cakes

Serve these tasty little patties as appetizers or make them into larger cakes for an entree.

2	*cups cooked chick-peas*
2	*cups mashed potatoes*
1	*cup thinly sliced scallions*
¼	*cup low-fat mayonnaise*
1	*tablespoon ground coriander or no-salt seasoning mixture Salt and pepper to taste*
¼	*cup flour or fine cracker crumbs*
2	*to **4** tablespoons vegetable oil*

Place the chick-peas in a blender or food processor and puree. Combine in a large bowl with the mashed potatoes, scallions, mayonnaise, coriander, and salt and pepper. Mix thoroughly. Form into small or large cakes, and roll in the flour or cracker crumbs. Heat 1 to 2 tablespoons of oil in a large skillet and fry 2 to 3 minutes a side over medium heat, until golden brown. Repeat until all cakes are cooked. Serve immediately or keep warm in a low oven.

Preparation time: 15 minutes
Cooking time: 5 minutes
Yield: 24 appetizers or 8 large cakes

Pasta Salad with Cannellini Beans and Red Peppers is a dish that can be made in a flash and will satisfy even the heartiest of appetites.

EGGPLANT

SOLANUM MELONGENA, FAMILY SOLANACEAE

Although native to southern Asia, eggplants are grown throughout the world and come in a variety of colors, shapes, and sizes. The most familiar are the large, bulbous, deep purple Italian varieties. These eggplants, also called *aubergine* and *melazine*, are associated with Mediterranean dishes like ratatouille, caponata, moussaka, baba ghanoush, and imam bayildi. Some Asian and Middle Eastern varieties resemble white and even green golfballs, while others are long and thin with colors that range from pink-lavender to lavender-on-white to green. Eggplants contain only small amounts of vitamins and minerals.

BUYING AND STORING

Available year-round, a fresh eggplant should have a glossy, unblemished skin and be firm to the touch. Store in a plastic bag in the refrigerator vegetable drawer and use within a few days.

PREPARATION

Mature fruits of the large dark purple Italian eggplant contain bitter juices. Many other varieties do not have bitter juices. To remove them, cut off the stem end, peel thinly, and slice or dice the eggplant. Place in a colander and sprinkle each piece with salt. Allow to drain for 20 to 30 minutes. Rinse under cold water and blot dry.

Eggplant flesh absorbs oil like a sponge. To avoid this, brown in a nonstick skillet for 5 to 10 minutes. Remove to a plate. Heat 1 to 2 tablespoons of oil and chopped garlic in the skillet, add the browned eggplant, and sauté for 5 minutes.

You can also brush raw eggplant slices with oil and broil or grill for 5 minutes on each side, or bake for 15 to 20 minutes at 350° F.

To prepare a large eggplant for mashing into dips, boil 15 minutes, bake 30 minutes, microwave 7 minutes, or broil or grill 3 to 5 minutes each quarter turn. (The flesh is most flavorful when the skin is blistered or charred.) Cool the eggplant under cold water. Remove the skin and gently squeeze the eggplant to remove the bitter juice. Place in a food processor or blender and puree with 2 tablespoons olive oil, 2 cloves garlic, 2 tablespoons lemon juice, and salt and pepper to taste. For baba ghanoush, add ¼ cup tahini (sesame seed paste).

To fry eggplant slices to serve as a side dish, leave the skin intact and cut into ½-inch-thick slices. Place the slices on paper towels, sprinkle with salt, and cover with a heavy kettle filled with water. This method forces out more juice. After 30 minutes, remove the weight, rinse the slices under cold water, and blot dry. Dip in flour (then in beaten egg and bread crumbs, if desired) and sauté in a little hot oil in a skillet over medium heat for 3 to 5 minutes on each side, until golden brown.

Fusilli Pasta Twists with Eggplant Tandoori

Serve this pasta hot or toss the sauce with the pasta and refrigerate overnight. Once the flavors have melded together, this is a flavorful dish to serve at room temperature.

1	*pound tricolor fusilli twists*
2	*tablespoons vegetable oil*
1	*cup finely chopped onion*
6	*cloves garlic, finely minced*
1	*pound eggplant, unpeeled and cut in ½-inch cubes (about 2½ cups)*
1	*tablespoon ground coriander*
1	*teaspoon turmeric*
1	*teaspoon cumin*
1	*teaspoon ground ginger*
½	*teaspoon black pepper*
1½	*cups plain yogurt*
	Cilantro leaves for garnish

Bring water to a boil in a 4-quart pan and cook the pasta as recommended on the packet. Simultaneously, heat oil in a large nonstick skillet over medium heat, add the onion, and sauté 5 minutes. Add the garlic and eggplant cubes and sprinkle the spices evenly over the top. Stir to combine and sauté for 10 minutes, turning the vegetables once in a while. Remove from the heat and stir in the yogurt. Drain the pasta and toss with the eggplant sauce. Serve immediately or refrigerate.

Preparation time: 15 minutes
Cooking time: 15 minutes
Yield: 4 servings

Eggplant Sandwiches can be eaten any time of day.

Eggplant Sandwiches

These sandwiches are perfect to serve at a brunch. Assemble early on and dip in the egg and bread crumbs just before frying in a skillet.

1	*large eggplant, unpeeled and cut into 12 ½-inch rounds*
2	*large tomatoes cut into ¼-inch-thick slices, not including the ends*
6	*slices of cheese (Muenster, provolone, Swiss), cut to fit eggplant rounds*
¼	*cup all-purpose flour*
2	*large eggs*
¼	*cup skim milk*
	Freshly ground pepper to taste
¾	*cup seasoned-cracker crumbs*
1	*tablespoon olive oil*

Place a large nonstick skillet over low-to-medium heat. Arrange the eggplant slices, 6 or so at a time, and lightly brown 1 side only for about 2 minutes. Remove and repeat until all slices have been browned on 1 side. Fit the tomato and cheese slices on the browned sides of 6 eggplant rounds. Top with the remaining 6 rounds with the browned side inwards. Sprinkle the flour onto a plate and dust each side of the eggplant sandwiches. Beat the eggs, skim milk, and pepper in a shallow pan large enough to hold the eggplant sandwiches. Turn the sandwiches over and thoroughly coat the other side. Remove and carefully set on a plate containing the cracker crumbs.

Turn once to coat both sides. Heat the oil in the large nonstick skillet over medium heat. When hot, arrange the sandwiches, leaving room to turn them over easily (it may be necessary to cook these in 2 batches, keeping the first 3 or so warm in a low-temperature oven). Cook 3 to 5 minutes on each side, or until nicely browned. Remove to individual plates and serve with a salad (and a knife and fork).

Preparation time: 15 minutes
Cooking time: 15 minutes
Yield: 4 to 6 servings

ENDIVE

CICHORIUM ENDIVA

Belgian or French endive is a relative of the blue flowering wild chicory, or succory, plant and is native to the Mediterranean area. Chicory was originally cultivated for its long root, which when pulled, dried, and ground, was made into a coffee-flavored drink. During the early 1800s, a Belgium gardener discovered that this root produced succulent cones of tightly furled white leaves (chicons) when wintered over in soil in a dark cellar. The Flemish name for this vegetable is *witloof*, which means "white leaf." In France, it is known simply as "endive."

BUYING AND STORING

Belgian endive is available from early autumn into late spring. For the mildest tasting chicons, choose those that are about 5 inches long and have creamy white, narrow, tightly formed leaves with light yellow tips. Loose leaves with dark tips indicate a strong flavor.

Store endive for up to 1 week in a plastic bag in the refrigerator vegetable drawer. Do not immerse in water or cut in half until ready to use.

PREPARATION

Like all chicories, the flavor of Belgian endive is slightly bitter. Removing about 1 half-inch of the inner core from the bottom helps to eliminate some of the bitterness of the larger, more mature endives. Other ideas include soaking in cold water with salt and vinegar, or dropping into boiling water for one minute, then plunging into ice-cold water.

In Mediterranean countries, endive is eaten regularly as a cooked vegetable. A very simple and delicious method is to cut the chicons in half lengthwise, sprinkle with olive oil and chopped garlic, broil or grill, and drizzle with balsamic vinegar to serve. You can also steam them whole and serve with butter and lemon juice or place in a dish, cover with a cheese sauce and grated Parmesan, and bake until bubbly. Their crisp quality also makes them ideal for stir-frying with scallions, shallots, or leeks and lots of garlic. When eaten raw, the leaves make an attractive addition to a salad composé and taste even better when dressed with a mustard vinaigrette. You can also stuff them with mashed blue cheese or a soft cheese flavored with herbs and serve them as an appetizer.

Stuffed Endive

The boat-shaped leaves of Belgian endive are perfect for stuffing with a simple blue-cheese spread or something as fancy as cooked shrimp and cream cheese.

2   *heads Belgian endive, separated into about 20 leaves*

Filling #1
1   *7-ounce can tuna in spring water, drained*
2   *tablespoons chunky peanut butter*
2   *tablespoons toasted sesame seeds*
2   *tablespoons soy sauce*
2   *tablespoons plain yogurt*

½   *cup finely minced scallions*
1   *clove garlic, crushed*
1   *teaspoon grated fresh ginger root*

Place all the ingredients except the endive leaves into a medium mixing bowl and mash them together with a fork. Stuff into the endive leaves and chill. Serve as an appetizer or a starter course.

Filling #2
3   *cups plain yogurt*
½   *cup finely minced scallions*
2   *cloves garlic, crushed*
½   *cup chopped walnuts*
     Salt and pepper to taste
1   *teaspoon finely chopped fresh sage leaves or ¼ teaspoon crumbled dried*

Line a colander with at least 3 layers of cheesecloth that are large enough to hang over the edges. Set into a bowl and spoon in the yogurt. Fold the extra cheesecloth over the top and refrigerate for several hours. The longer it drains, the thicker the yogocheese. Reduce the yogurt to about 1½ cups. Transfer the yogocheese to a medium-size mixing bowl and stir in the rest of the ingredients. Spoon into the endive leaves and chill. Serve as an appetizer or a starter course.

Preparation time: 20 minutes
Yield: 20 appetizers or
10 first-course servings

Crisp endive leaves make suitable containers for vegetable and herb mixtures, mashed beans, or flaked fish.

FOENICULUM VULGARE VAR. DULCE, FAMILY UMBELLIFERAE

Fennel, sometimes called *finocchio* or Florentine fennel, is native to Mediterranean countries. Cultivated since Roman times, it has long been prized for its medicinal qualities as well as its many culinary uses. From the thick layers of its white, bulbous base to its thin stalks, and from its green, feathery, dill-like leaves to its seeds, this anise-flavored vegetable is totally edible.

NUTRITIONAL VALUE
Don't count on this white vegetable to boost vitamin intake. Use it to add bulk, texture, and flavor to a variety of dishes.

BUYING AND STORING
Fennel grows above ground and develops a strong licorice-flavored, dark green, bulbous base. To induce a blanched white color and a sweet, mild flavor, the bulbs are covered with soil or straw.

A cool-weather crop, fennel is widely available for most of the year. It is usually sold in a creamy white form with the top fronds cut off. Store in a plastic bag in the vegetable drawer of the refrigerator for 4 to 5 days.

PREPARATION
If the leaves are still attached, remove, chop, and add to sauces to accompany fish, boiled potatoes, lima beans, cauliflower, or any food that needs a little zip of flavor. Fish grilled over a bed of fresh leaves will be subtly flavored with anise.

Trim the stalks to just above the bulb. The crisp layers and stalks are crunchy and ideal for slicing or grating to eat raw in a salad. Or reserve the stalks and spread with soft cheese, or slice and add to a vegetable stir-fry. Cut a thin slice off the bottom of the bulb and remove damaged or browned outer layer. These pieces can be added to the soup or stock pot for a delicate flavor. Slice 4 bulbs in half vertically, place them in a single layer in a baking dish, add ¼ cup of water, cover with plastic wrap, and microwave on high for 10 minutes. Drain, season with pepper, sprinkle with ¼ cup grated cheese, and place under broiler for 2 minutes, until bubbly.

Curried Fennel and Apple Salad

This salad is as delicious as it is pretty.

½	*cup low-fat mayonnaise*
2	*tablespoons lime juice*
1	*teaspoon grated lime rind*
2	*teaspoons curry powder*
1	*tablespoon prepared honey mustard*
1	*fennel bulb, trimmed of stalks and leaves, diced (about 1 cup)*
2	*large apples (crispin, golden delicious, or jonagold), diced (about 2 cups)*
1	*large red, orange, or yellow bell pepper, diced (about 1¼ cups)*
1	*head radicchio, separated into leaves*

Combine the mayonnaise, lime juice, rind, curry, and honey mustard in a small bowl. Place the diced fennel, apples, and bell pepper in a large bowl and mix with ¼ cup of the curry mayonnaise. Refrigerate if desired and allow flavors to blend. Arrange 2 leaves of radicchio on individual plates and spoon the vegetables on top. Serve the remaining mayonnaise separately.

Note: Instead of radicchio, serve it on bibb or buttercrunch lettuce leaves, or tender cabbage leaves, or stuffed into large tomatoes.

Preparation time: 20 minutes
Yield: 4 servings

Chilled Fennel Soup

This chilled soup can be made ahead as a starter for a dinner or a special lunch.

2 *tablespoons olive oil*
2 *fennel bulbs, trimmed of leaves and stalks, thinly sliced*
1 *medium onion, thinly sliced*
1 *large potato, thinly sliced*
2 *cloves garlic, finely minced*
4 *cups vegetable stock or water with bouillon cube*
      Salt and pepper to taste
1 *tablespoon fresh lemon thyme leaves or chopped lemon balm leaves*
2 *cups (16 ounces) nonfat lemon or plain yogurt*
      Leaves of bee balm or lemon balm or small tender sprigs of lemon thyme for garnish

Heat the oil in a heavy 3-quart saucepan over medium heat and add the fennel, onion, potato, and garlic. Stir and sauté for 5 minutes. Add the vegetable stock, salt, and pepper and bring to a boil. Reduce the heat, cover the pot, and simmer for 15 minutes, until the vegetables are tender. Puree the soup in at least 2 batches, in a blender or food processor. Pour into a soup tureen and allow to cool. Stir in the lemon thyme or chopped balm leaves. Add the yogurt, stir to combine, and chill. Garnish with whole leaves when ready to serve.

Preparation time: 20 minutes
Cooking time: 20 minutes
Yield: 4 servings

The combination of crisp, fresh vegetables in Curried Fennel and Apple Salad tastes just as delicious when served on a bed of Bibb lettuce or dark green spinach leaves.

GARLIC

ALLIUM SATIVUM, FAMILY LILIACEAE

The Egyptians worshiped garlic; the Greeks and Romans praised its healing powers, and throughout history, people all over the world have used it to control infections. The Romans fed raw garlic to their soldiers to give them strength. American settlers gave it to their livestock to keep illness at bay. It has been used to vanquish vampires, repel fleas, and bring good luck. In recent years, researchers have found that garlic contains alicin, a natural antibiotic.

Of the more than 300 varieties of garlic grown around the world, only a handful are grown commercially. These include two white-skinned varieties (one with large cloves forming a long head, the other with shorter, rounded cloves) and a purple-skinned garlic with small cloves forming a squat head. This is slightly milder than the whites, but not as mild or as nutty-flavored as the elephant garlic (*Allium scordoprasum*), which is not a true garlic at all. Elephant garlic cloves are at least three times bigger than those of the largest white garlic varieties (one clove can weigh up to three ounces) and are encased in thick, cream-colored skins, which are easy to remove.

NUTRITIONAL VALUE

Studies have shown that the daily consumption of between 7 and 28 cloves of raw garlic may help prevent cholesterol buildup and stomach cancer. While using one or two cloves a day may not have the same effect, garlic in this quantity can work miracles on bland food.

BUYING AND STORING

Choose plump, firm heads of garlic with papery skins intact. Store in the refrigerator in plastic bags for 3 to 4 weeks. In the autumn, look for garlic braids at the farmers markets. Store uncovered in a cool, dry, well-ventilated place for up to 4 months. For long storage, peel the cloves and cover with vinegar. Cloves covered with olive oil have been found to release a toxic chemical, so store them in an airtight container in the refrigerator and use within 1 to 2 days. Although sprouted bulbs have a milder flavor, they are still good to eat. (The "sprout" tastes bitter so split the clove open and remove the green shoot.) They are also perfect for planting in the garden or in a pot on the windowsill.

PREPARATION

Separate a bulb (cluster or head) of garlic into individual cloves. To make peeling easier, drop into hot water for a few seconds, or lay a clove on a flat surface and press it down hard with the flat side of a large kitchen knife.

The way garlic is prepared affects the flavor. Crushing it in a press releases the oil and the strongest flavor. When minced with a sharp knife, it retains a sharp taste without the bite; sautéed quickly over high heat, its potency is sealed in. When just a subtle flavor of garlic is desired, use sliced or whole flattened cloves and cook slowly or add to a sauce or stew. Another way to add delicate flavor is to take a cut clove of garlic and rub it around the salad bowl or over hot toast, or sauté it in oil and then remove before adding the rest of the recipe's ingredients.

To chop garlic, flatten peeled cloves of garlic on a cutting surface. Place the blade of a small (7-inch) chef's knife approximately at the center of the clove. Hold the handle of the knife firmly in one hand, and with the fingers of the other hand on top of the knife at the tip, swing the knife up and down and then back and forth. The bottom tip of the knife should remain pressed down with the fingers in the same spot. Use the knife to push the garlic back towards the center of the cutting area. Continue cutting until the garlic is chopped or minced finely.

Garlic Rouille

Made with sweet and hot red peppers and redolent with garlic, this spicy sauce is served with a variety of soups in France. It is especially wonderful with a chunky fish soup like bouillabaisse; spread on oven-toasted French bread that has been drizzled with olive oil and rubbed with a cut clove of garlic; or spooned over boiled potatoes.

3   *large cloves garlic*
1   *large red pepper, seeds removed, roasted, and skinned*
1   *hot red chile pepper, about 2 inches long, stem removed and seeds intact*
1   *slice white bread*
2   *tablespoons Asian fish sauce or fish soup broth (or water)*
½   *cup olive oil*

Place the garlic in a food processor or blender and puree. Add the rest of the ingredients and puree until smooth.

Preparation time: 15 minutes
Yield: ¾ cup

Garlic's distinct flavor has made it a worldwide favorite; many famous dishes would not be the same without it.

Herbed Garlic Cheese

Make this herbed garlic in 10 minutes when friends drop by unexpectedly.

8 ounces low-fat Neufchâtel cream cheese or soft farmers' cheese
3 cloves garlic, crushed
1 teaspoon dried thyme leaves
1 teaspoon dried oregano leaves
½ teaspoon dried tarragon leaves
1 tablespoon chopped chives or finely chopped scallion greens
¼ cup chopped parsley leaves or **2** teaspoons cracked pepper or **2** teaspoons paprika

Cream the cheese in a mixing bowl and beat in the garlic, thyme, oregano, tarragon, and chives. Form into a log or a ball and roll in the chopped parsley, pepper, or paprika. Refrigerate until firm. Serve with crackers, French bread, or celery.

Note: Reduce the fat in this recipe by substituting yogocheese for the cream cheese. To make yogocheese: line a metal sieve with double layers of cheesecloth and suspend over a deep bowl. Spoon 16 ounces of nonfat plain yogurt into the lines sieve, refrigerate and allow to drip overnight. The result is one cup of yogocheese.

Preparation time: 10 minutes
Yield: 8 ounces cheese

Herbed Garlic Cheese can be stuffed into crepes or jumbo pasta shells.

LEEKS

ALLIUM AMPELOPRASUM (ALSO A. PORRUM), FAMILY LILIACEAE

The ancient Greeks called leeks *prason*. To the Romans, leeks were known as *porrum*, and Pliny said that the best ones came from Egypt. Spreading from the eastern Mediterranean countries during the Middle Ages, leeks became popular in Europe, particularly in France and Britain. The Welsh adopted the leek as their national emblem after their soldiers wore them as identification badges during a sixth-century war in which they defeated the Anglo-Saxons. Early settlers transported this famous *Allium* to America. As members of the *Allium* genus, leeks are related to onions, but these giant scallion look-alikes are much sweeter and milder than most onion varieties.

NUTRITIONAL VALUE
One whole, raw leek, green and white parts, weighing 4 ounces, offers moderate amounts of vitamins A and C, folacin, magnesium, phosphorus, calcium, and potassium. When cooked, it loses 50 percent of its nutrients.

BUYING AND STORING
Once considered a speciality item in the United States, leeks are now available for up to eight months of the year—they are easy to grow, suffer from few insect or disease problems, are sufficiently cold resistant, and can be harvested over a long period.

Choose leeks with fresh, green tops and crisp white "necks," which should

Leeks are the refined cousins of the stronger-flavored onions. Wash between each layer to remove all traces of soil.

Baked Fish and Leeks in Yogurt

be about 1 inch in diameter and glistening white for 3 inches or so from the root ends. Wilted, yellowish tops are an indication of tough, woody necks.

Stored in perforated plastic bags in a refrigerator, leeks remain fresh for approximately two months. Washed leeks can be blotted dry and refrigerated in a plastic bag for up to 4 days.

PREPARATION

Trim the tops and cut off the root end about ¼ inch above where it joins the white part. (Plant these roots in a pot of soil or in the garden and they will grow into mature leeks.) With the point of a small knife, cut out the cone-shaped core from the bottom. It is usually necessary to remove the two outermost leaves or at least cut them off where the color changes from yellowish green to dark green. It is not unusual to find sandy soil lodged between the leaves as a result of mounding earth around the leeks to blanch the necks. Split the leeks lengthwise and wash thoroughly in cold running water to remove any particles of soil remaining between the leaves. Blot dry and slice fine, chop, or leave whole, depending on the recipe. Leeks cook quickly—steam or braise them in a little water for 10 to 15 minutes.

Leeks' distinctive flavor makes them particularly desirable for flavoring pureed soups like potato, pumpkin, and cauliflower; fish dishes and custards; quiches; and soufflés. When braised or roasted, they need no adornment except a shake of pepper. However, covered with a little cream sauce and a sprin-

kling of grated Parmesan cheese and popped under the broiler, they are converted into a dish fit for kings. Leeks are also delicious steamed, marinated in vinaigrette, and served chilled.

Leeks Vinaigrette

Serve the leeks alone or combine with asparagus, green beans, or Belgian endive. Instead of simmering the leeks in water, try broiling or grilling for added flavor.

4	*leeks*
½	*cup Classic or Low-Fat Vinaigrette (page 115)*
4	*Boston lettuce leaves*

Trim the leeks to about 8 inches long. Cut in half lengthwise but not through the root end. Wash thoroughly. Bring water to a boil in a 2- to 3-quart saucepan. Add the leeks, reduce the heat, and cover the pan. Simmer for 15 minutes, until the leeks are tender. Drain in a colander. After draining, blot the leeks dry and cut right through the root end. Brush with olive oil and grill or broil 4 to 6 inches from the heat for 10 minutes, turning once halfway through. They should be slightly charred and tender. Arrange the leeks in a single layer in a shallow dish and pour the vinaigrette over the top. Cover and refrigerate until chilled. Arrange the lettuce on a serving platter and place a leek in each leaf. Spoon dressing over top.

Preparation time: 15 minutes
Cooking time: 25 minutes
Yield: 4 servings

4	*fish fillets—cod, mahi-mahi, haddock, or monkfish (about 1¾ pounds)*
2	*teaspoons chopped fresh tarragon or dill or 1 teaspoon dried*
4	*leeks, cleaned and cut in ¼-inch slices (about 4 cups)*
1	*tablespoon olive oil*
2	*cloves garlic, minced*
6	*ounces small mushrooms, sliced*
8	*ounces plain yogurt*
¼	*cup light cream*
1	*tablespoon cornstarch*
¼	*teaspoon each salt and white pepper*
1	*tablespoon paprika for garnish*

Preheat the oven to 325° F.

Rinse and blot dry the fish fillets and arrange in a single layer in an ovenproof dish. Sprinkle with the tarragon and cover with the sliced leeks. Heat the oil in a skillet over medium heat and sauté the garlic and mushrooms for 3 minutes. Spoon over the leeks. Combine the yogurt, cream, cornstarch, salt, and pepper in a jug and pour over the top. Place in the middle of the oven and bake for 20 minutes, until the leeks are tender and the fish flakes.

Note: The oven temperature needs to be low to avoid curdling the yogurt.

Preparation time: 15 minutes
Cooking time: 20 minutes
Yield: 4 servings

Use only tender young leeks or the inner leaves of older leeks for Leeks Vinaigrette.

Mushrooms are the fleshy fruiting bodies of fungi that, in true fungi fashion, feed on organic matter. They grow wherever the soil is rich and moist, and where there are leaves or pine needles underfoot and shady boughs above. They also grow on decaying logs, on trees, near the base of trees, in fields, by the roadside, and on dung. Wild edible mushrooms grow in most countries throughout the world. In North America there are about 50 edible varieties, while in Europe, over 300 varieties are picked in the wild. To go collecting in the wild you need a mushroom guide book because many poisonous fungi resemble edible species.

During the last decade, mushrooms have moved into the spotlight and it is now possible to buy several varieties of cultivated "wild" mushrooms in the supermarkets. During the spring, mushrooms harvested from the wild are available in many of the specialty markets. Exports from Europe, China, and Japan include dried, canned, and pickled mushrooms.

Brown Mushrooms
Agaricus bisporus

Like the cultivated white, the cultivated brown mushroom is a subspecies of the field (or meadow) mushroom (*Agaricus campestris*). This brown-capped fungus also grows abundantly in the wilds of Italy and has been a longtime favorite in Italian restaurants. For this reason, cultivated brown mushrooms are often marketed as cremini, portobello, or Roman. The flattish caps, usually harvested at a mature stage, are more flavorful than that of the common white mushroom.

Cep Mushrooms
Boletus edulis

Called *porcini* (por-chee-nee) in Italy, *cepe* (sep) in France, and king bolete or cep in North America, this wild mushroom is available fresh during spring and summer. Short and thick, cream-colored stems are topped with rounded, closed, orangish-brown caps. The firm texture and meaty flavor make them an all-purpose mushroom. Also available dried.

Chanterelle Mushrooms
Cantharellus cibarius

Found growing wild in European and North American woods, these tiny, trumpet-shaped mushrooms have a

Brown or Cremini mushrooms are m *flavorful than the common cream-colored* ***cap mushrooms.***

slightly fruity or peppery flavor depending on the subspecies' color, which ranges from orange-yellow to purple-black to pale gold. Chanterelles, or girolles as they are also called, are available fresh only in limited quantities during late summer and autumn. The firm flesh is rendered softer when gently stewed or braised. Also sold canned and dried.

Common Cultivated Mushrooms
Agaricus bisporus

This is the most common mushroom and is harvested at three stages: button, medium-size rounded cup, and flat or open. With its creamy white skin and light brown gills, this mushroom has a delicate flavor, which intensifies as it matures. The cultivated variety of the field or meadow mushroom (*Agaricus campestris*) is available year-round. Use in any recipe calling for mushrooms.

Enoki Mushrooms
Flammulina vulutipes

These tiny, white mushrooms with their long, thin stems and miniature caps have a very delicate flavor. They grow wild and are also cultivated in Japan and California. Also called *enokidake* and velvet stem, they are harvested in clusters from the wet pads on which they are grown. When ready to use, cut them off one inch above the pad. They are too fragile for cooked dishes unless stir-fried or dropped into broth at the last minute. Use enoki to dress up a salad or slip into a sandwich, where their mild flavor can be appreciated.

Morel Mushrooms
Morchella

Although a patent is pending for their culture, morels have so far defied the final steps of commercial cultivation. However, they grow prolifically in the wild in many regions of North America and Europe. Those most commonly harvested are *Morchella esculenta* (yellow) and *Morchella elata* (black). Morels are available fresh in specialty stores from April to June, and year-round in dried form. The hollow, ridged "honeycomb" caps are nutty flavored and intensely aromatic. They are particularly delicious when incorporated in cream sauces.

Oyster Mushrooms
Pleurotus ostreatus

These wild mushrooms are being increasingly cultivated and are harvested ... g from one to several ... fan shaped cap is creamy white to grayish blue with creamy gills. The smooth texture has a delicate, salty flavor—hence their "oyster" name. Delicious sautéed or braised.

Shiitake Mushrooms
Lentinus edodes

For centuries these mushrooms have been cultivated in Japan and China and only recently widely cultivated in the rest of the world. Now available fresh or dried year-round, shiitake (or golden oak) mushrooms are large and meaty with brown caps and creamy gills. Extremely flavorful, they are easy to grow on oak or hornbean logs, which are left to age in the partial shade of a woodlot. Excellent for slicing and stir-frying, grilling or sautéeing, shiitakes are a tasty addition to soups and sauces.

NUTRITIONAL VALUE

The meaty flesh of mushrooms is high in water content and also high in protein—a 3-ounce serving has 2 grams of protein. They contain a trace of calcium, iron, magnesium, vitamin C, and some folacin. They are a good source of phosphorus and are particularly high in potassium.

BUYING AND STORING

Select mushrooms with firm, unblemished tops. Mushroom caps should feel damp and fresh. Reject either shiny or wrinkled ones that have started to dry out. Also, when purchasing those encased in plastic, there should be no visible moisture. Wet or cream-colored mushrooms that have turned brown will taste strong and bitter. Store mushrooms in a paper bag in the refrigerator and use within a few days of purchase. To store mushrooms for several months, slice or quarter and sauté in a little olive oil over medium heat for approximately 5 minutes. Cool, enclose in an airtight container, and freeze.

PREPARATION

When mushrooms are firm and fresh, they do not need washing or peeling. Simply wipe off the dirt with a damp kitchen towel.

Use very fresh mushrooms when eating them raw in a salad. When a cooked but fresh flavor is desired, sauté or stir-fry over medium-high heat for 2 to 3 minutes to retain their firm texture. When cooked slowly in a sauce, soup, or casserole, they become soft and impart their flavor to the contents of the dish.

Mushroom and Basil Salad

Available year-round, button mushrooms are perfect for mixing with seasonal greens like spinach, crunchy butterhead lettuce, green beans, and snow peas. In the winter, toss in a cupful of shredded carrots and parsnips, blanched broccoli, julienned slices of turnip, or tiny brussels sprouts.

1	pound button mushrooms, thinly sliced
1	medium-size red bell pepper, diced small
½	cup olive oil
3	tablespoons balsamic vinegar
2	cloves garlic, crushed
1	teaspoon dry mustard
2	tablespoons finely chopped fresh chives
¼	cup chopped fresh basil leaves
	Freshly ground black pepper

Place the sliced mushrooms and diced pepper in a serving bowl. Combine the oil, vinegar, garlic, and dry mustard in a screw-top jar and shake vigorously. Pour over the mushrooms and pepper and toss together. Allow to marinate for several hours. Sprinkle the chives and basil over the mushroom mixture. Add ground pepper to taste and stir gently to combine. Garnish with basil leaves.

Preparation time: 15 minutes
Yield: 4 servings

Most mushroom varieties are interchangeable. Using them as the main vegetable in a dish allows their subtle but distinct flavor to be fully appreciated, as in Mushroom and Basil Salad, Mushroom Soup, or Mushroom Stroganoff (opposite page).

Mushroom Soup

Serve this soup with a goat cheese and arugula salad and whole wheat biscuits or scones.

3	tablespoons olive oil or sweet butter
1	pound fresh, flat Cremini or shiitake mushrooms, sliced (about 6 cups)
1	large onion, chopped (about 1 cup)
2	cloves garlic, minced
2	tablespoons all-purpose flour
1	cup vegetable stock
1½	cups low-fat milk
1	cup nonfat plain yogurt
	Salt and pepper to taste
1	to 2 tablespoons chopped fennel leaves

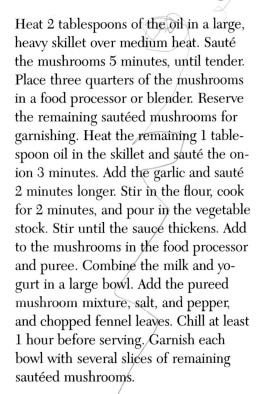

Heat 2 tablespoons of the oil in a large, heavy skillet over medium heat. Sauté the mushrooms 5 minutes, until tender. Place three quarters of the mushrooms in a food processor or blender. Reserve the remaining sautéed mushrooms for garnishing. Heat the remaining 1 tablespoon oil in the skillet and sauté the onion 3 minutes. Add the garlic and sauté 2 minutes longer. Stir in the flour, cook for 2 minutes, and pour in the vegetable stock. Stir until the sauce thickens. Add to the mushrooms in the food processor and puree. Combine the milk and yogurt in a large bowl. Add the pureed mushroom mixture, salt, and pepper, and chopped fennel leaves. Chill at least 1 hour before serving. Garnish each bowl with several slices of remaining sautéed mushrooms.

Note: If a hot mushroom soup is preferred, substitute milk for the yogurt and add with the rest of the milk.

Preparation time: 10 minutes
Cooking time: 20 minutes
Yield: 4 servings

Mushroom Stroganoff

Serve this stroganoff as a side dish, as an entree on toast, over rice, or as a sauce for pasta.

2	tablespoons olive oil
1	large onion, chopped (about 1 cup)
2	to 4 cloves garlic, finely minced
½	cup tomato sauce
1	tablespoon mild paprika
12	ounces mushrooms, sliced (about 3 cups)
	Salt and pepper to taste
¾	cup low-fat sour cream
¼	cup chopped parsley

Heat the oil in a large skillet over medium heat and sauté the onions for 5 minutes. Add the garlic and sauté 1 minute. Stir in the tomato sauce, paprika, and the mushrooms. Cover the skillet, reduce the heat to low, and simmer for 15 minutes, stirring once or twice. Remove the skillet from the heat, stir in the salt, pepper, and sour cream. Transfer to a serving platter or spoon over toast, rice, or pasta and sprinkle with parsley. Serve immediately.

Note: For a pasta sauce, increase the tomato sauce and sour cream to 1 cup each.

Preparation time: 15 minutes
Cooking time: 20 minutes
Yield: 4 servings

OKRA

A tropical plant native to Africa, okra, or gumbo as it is also called, is a staple in some parts of the world. In India, it is known as *bindi*, in the Middle East, it is *bamia*, and in Europe and Commonwealth countries, it goes by the name "lady's finger." In the United States, it is an essential ingredient in southern gumbo, a stew thickened with the mucilaginous pods of okra. Although okra is grown for its finger-length, green, pointed pods, the large, pale yellow flowers with their purple hearts could take their place in the ornamental garden. Like all hibiscus flowers, they last one day and are quickly replaced with pods.

NUTRITIONAL VALUE

Okra has a high water-content and is a moderate source of calcium, magnesium, phosphorus, potassium, folacin, and vitamins A and C.

BUYING AND STORING

Available most of the year, okra is at its freshest and tenderest during summer. Choose pods that are small, unblemished, and bright green. Older pods are tough and stringy.

Store in a plastic bag in the vegetable drawer of the refrigerator and use within 3 days.

PREPARATION

The pods are picked when they are from 2 to 4 inches long, then sliced or left whole to cook in sautés of mixed vegetables, soups, and stews. Small, tender pods are the best for pickling whole. Larger pods are good for breading and deep-frying.

Okra releases a gelatinous substance when sliced or cooked slowly. It is this gluey quality that makes it ideal for thickening gumbos or stews. However, if the pod is left intact and cooked quickly, the texture will not break down. A dash of vinegar or lemon juice added to the okra also helps to cut the slipperiness, which develops after about twenty minutes of slow cooking.

Wash the pods, trim the stem without cutting into the cap, add to a stir-fry of vegetables, and cook over medium-high heat for 5 minutes. You can also steam the pods for 8 to 10 minutes and dress with a shallot vinaigrette. Very small pods are deliciously crunchy; wash and toss raw into a salad for a treat.

Kosher Dill Pickled Okra

Don't even attempt to make these pickles with mature okra pods—you need tiny tender ones.

3	pounds 2-inch-long okra pods, washed and stems removed
12	whole cloves garlic, peeled
12	hot 2-inch-long chile peppers, washed and stems removed
12	dill sprigs
12	celery leaves
3	cups water
3	cups white vinegar
1	tablespoon kosher salt

Arrange the okra in hot, clean jars, alternating the pointed and flat ends. Add one of each of the garlic cloves, chile peppers, dill, and celery leaves to every jar. Bring the water, vinegar, and salt to a rolling boil and pour into the prepared jars, leaving a ½-inch head space. Screw the tops on tightly and process 5 minutes in a boiling-water bath. Remove the jars with tongs and cool on a wire rack. The flavor develops fully after 1 month.

Preparation time: 10 minutes
Cooking time: 10 minutes
Yield: 12 cups

Okra Salad with Tomatoes and Basil

For this salad, use the freshest and smallest okra you can find.

1   *pound small okra pods, with stems removed*

3   *large shallots, chopped (about ⅓ cup)*

½   *cup Classic or Low-Fat Vinaigrette (page 115)*

1   *pound cherry tomatoes, cut in half*

½   *cup chopped fresh basil leaves*

6   *to **8** large Boston lettuce leaves*

Cook okra in boiling water for 4 to 5 minutes, until tender. Drain, turn the okra into a large mixing bowl, and toss it with chopped shallots and vinaigrette. Refrigerate until cool. Combine with the cherry tomatoes and basil. Arrange the lettuce leaves on individual plates and top with the okra salad.

Preparation time: 15 minutes
Yield: 6 to 8 servings

Okra Salad is a classic combination of okra and tomatoes, but try substituting sliced sweet peppers or purple French beans cooked al dente.

As one of the world's oldest cultivated vegetables, onions have been used to flavor foods and cure ills for over 4,000 years. The onion family includes not only sweet Vidalia, Texas Grano, Bermuda, Spanish, mellow yellow, and acrid white onions, but the all-time flavoring favorites like leeks, scallions, garlic, and chives.

Throughout history, these members of the onion family have provided health-protecting remedies. The Welsh wore them on their chests when they defeated the Saxons during the sixth century. In the eighteenth century, Captain James Cook made each of his men eat 30 pounds of onions as a safeguard against scurvy while on long sea voyages. During the U.S. Civil War, General Ulysses S. Grant refused to move camp until he received a trainload of onions to feed his men.

BULB ONIONS
ALLIUM CEPA

Strong Yellow Onions
There are several varieties of yellow onions. While some are globe-shaped, others are elongated, but they all have firm or hard flesh. Covered with dry golden skin, the flesh ranges from white to yellowish white and the flavor from mild to pungent. Slicing into onions with hard, pungent flesh releases a strong chemical that affects the cornea. Onions with an abundance of this chemical are the best storers and for that reason are available year-round. The sizes range from 2 to 16 ounces. These basic cooking onions can be boiled, baked, fried, steamed, and added to soups and stews.

Strong White Onions
These vary in size from the tiny pearl onions to the larger golf-ball size to those that weigh 8 ounces. They have

Onions come in a variety of shapes, sizes, colors, and flavors.

firm to hard flesh and vary in intensity from strong to extremely pungent. Use large whites as all-purpose cooking onions. Cook the smaller ones whole and add to a cream sauce or a boeuf bourguignonne, or caramelize them in oil or butter. The tiny pearls make great pickles. The smaller ones are easier to peel if they are first blanched. To do this, cut a shallow **X** across the root end and drop into boiling water for 1 minute.

Mild Onions

There are several varieties of mild onions available. Spanish onions are large, round, and white-fleshed, with golden yellow skin. Less common are the Spanish onions with purple-red skin and deep red flesh. Depending on where they are grown, they may be milder, sweeter, or stronger than others sold under the same name.

Bermuda onions are large, somewhat flat on the top and bottom, and have yellowish white flesh. Both Spanish and Bermuda onions are good for eating raw in salads and on sandwiches, and they are delicious when baked whole, sautéed, or stir-fried. Sometimes classified as sweet onions, their sugar content and bold flavor make them good contenders for onion soup—when sautéed slowly and for a long time, they caramelize and give the soup a rich golden brown color.

The large, round Italian red and the long, thin Torpedo red are very mellow onions. Chop them for salsas and salads; slice them in thin rings for sandwiches and garnishes. Add them to spaghetti sauces, soups, pizzas, and breads for a mild oniony flavor.

Sweet Onions

The sweetest onions are grown in regions where the soil is organically rich and low in sulphur. The best-known sweets include Georgia Vidalias, Hawaiian Mauis, California Imperial Sweets, Texas Sweeties, Washington Walla Wallas, and New Mexico Carzalias. These are all so mild and sweet they can be eaten raw like an apple. Delicious on sandwiches and in salads, they are also the best varieties for making into deep-fried onion rings. Such sweet onions are high in water-content and often weigh a pound. These onions are not suitable for long-term storage but, depending on the region and the variety, they are available fresh from March through August.

NUTRITIONAL VALUE

Bulb onions are the least nutritious member of the *Allium* family. However, they are said to cure colds, lower blood pressure, and cure many other ailments. They contain modest amounts of vitamin C, calcium, and potassium.

BUYING AND STORING

Whether fresh or out-of-storage, onions are available year-round. Look for firm-fleshed onions with dry, papery skins and no growth from the top or root area. Reject onions that are soft around the neck—an indication of a spoiled interior.

Store whole onions in newspaper or paper bags in a cool (just above freezing), dry, well-ventilated place. Onions that have been cut in half should be kept in a sealed plastic bag in the refrigerator. Sweet onions keep for a few months if wrapped individually in news-

paper and stored on the lower shelves of the refrigerator. Do not store onions and apples together. Apples emit ethylene gas, which causes onions to sprout.

PREPARATION

There are two good ways to avoid crying when peeling and chopping pungent onions: wear goggles to keep the eye-watering onion fumes from coming in contact with the cornea; or refrigerate the onion until it's cold, peel it under cold water, and then chop it in a food processor (but watch out for the fumes when removing the lid).

An easy way to chop an onion into uniform pieces is to cut it in half through the root and peel off the dry skin. Lay 1 half flat on a chopping surface and make 2 horizontal cuts from the neck end. Cut up to but not into the root. Make 5 or 6 vertical cuts lengthwise, turn the onion, and make several cuts across the width. Discard the root and repeat with the other half.

When flavoring a salad with raw onions, some of the pungency can be reduced by pouring boiling water over thin slices. Allow to stand for 2 minutes or so, drain off the water, and refrigerate to crisp up the slices.

SCALLIONS

ALLIUM CEPA OR
A. FISTULOSUM

Scallions are young onions harvested when the green tops are about 6 inches high and before the slender white root forms a bulb. However, there are varieties of bunching onions, or Japanese onions, as these pencil-thin onions are also called, that do not form bulbs.

NUTRITIONAL VALUE

Scallions are an excellent source of vitamin A and a good source of calcium, potassium, and vitamin C.

BUYING AND STORING

Scallions, or spring onions, are available year-round. Look for firm, white stems and crisp, green tops. Most produce stores trim and clean these onions, so just pack in plastic bags and refrigerate for up to 1 week. For longer storage, slice the entire stem or just the green part, pack into airtight plastic bags or rigid containers, and freeze.

PREPARATION

These pencil-thin onions are packed with flavor and are mild enough to eat raw. The green tops can be sliced and used in place of chives in dips, sauces, and salad dressings, and as a garnish for soups, chopped eggs, and potato dishes. Both green and white parts of the stem can be chopped and used in place of onions in many recipes or cut into 2-inch pieces and stir-fried with mixed vegetables. Thin slivers make a tasty addition to sandwiches, while the whole stems are a good replacement for pickled onions on a plate of ploughman's lunch, that traditional British lunch of a thick wedge of crumbly cheddar and a hunk of fresh bread.

Scallions look like a miniature version of leeks but have a much stronger bite.

©Bruce Byers/FPG International

SHALLOTS

ALLIUM ASCALONICUM,
FAMILY LILIACEAE

A close relative of garlic and onions, the shallot is believed to have been transported to Europe from Ascalon in Palestine by the Crusaders around the twelfth century. Like garlic, it belongs to the appregatum group and forms clusters containing several long, pickling-onion-size bulbs. Some French varieties are as large as chicken eggs and as mild as sweet granex onions. Underneath the copper-brown skin, the flavorful flesh is a pearly purple-gray.

BUYING AND STORING

Once available only during autumn and early winter, shallots can now be purchased year-round from supermarkets as well as specialty food stores. Select firm bulbs with dry skins and no blemishes. Stored in a nylon stocking and hung in a dry, cool, well-ventilated place, shallots will keep for months. For short-term storage, keep in the vegetable drawer of the refrigerator for up to two weeks. With their firm texture and mellow flavor, shallots are a good candidate for the pickle jar.

PREPARATION

Substitute shallots for onions when a subtle or sweet flavor is desired in cooked dishes. They do not affect the tear ducts and are easier to digest than onions. Peel and chop or slice for a mellow raw onion flavor in salad dressings, mayonnaises, or potato salads.

French Onion Soup

This classic soup is easy to prepare and is a crowd pleaser. The cheese turns it into a hearty dish.

3   tablespoons butter
1   tablespoon olive oil
2   pounds yellow onions, thinly sliced
5   cups beer
1   bay leaf
      Salt and pepper to taste
6   slices French bread, lightly toasted
1½ cups grated mozzarella or
      Swiss cheese

Heat the butter and oil in a heavy 4-quart saucepan over medium-high heat and sauté the onions (stirring frequently) 15 to 20 minutes, until golden brown and caramelized. Add the beer, bay leaf, salt, and pepper, cover the pot, and reduce the heat to low. Simmer for 25 minutes, until the onions are tender. Ladle the soup into ovenproof bowls, top with a slice of French bread, and sprinkle with ¼ cup of cheese. Place 6 inches under the broiler for 3 to 5 minutes, until the cheese is lightly browned and bubbly. Serve immediately.

Preparation time: 15 minutes
Cooking time: 55 minutes
Yield: 6 servings

Onion and Potato Gratin

Baked onions and potatoes are scrumptious. Serve them at a weekend breakfast or dinner anytime, accompanied by a vegetable and/or a salad.

2   large onions, peeled and sliced
      ¼ inch thick
4   large potatoes, scrubbed and sliced
      ¼ inch thick
2   tablespoons olive oil
2   tablespoons fresh thyme leaves
1   tablespoon fresh sage, chopped
      Salt and pepper to taste
¼   cup grated Parmesan cheese

Preheat the oven to 400° F.

Toss the potato slices in a bowl with the olive oil, thyme, sage, salt, and pepper. Arrange in overlapping layers with the onions in a large, shallow baking dish measuring about 10 × 12 inches. Sprinkle with the Parmesan cheese and bake for 45 minutes, until tender and golden brown. Serve immediately.

Note: If fresh thyme and sage are not available, substitute other fresh chopped herbs such as parsley and mint, or parsley and basil.

Preparation time: 15 minutes
Cooking time: 45 minutes
Yield: 4 servings

Shallot Sauce

Serve this delicious sauce on homemade pizza, toasted French bread, biscuits, baked potatoes, or steamed fish, or stuffed into omelettes and crepes.

2   pounds shallots, peeled and coarsely
      chopped (about 6 cups)
¼   cup margarine or butter
¼   cup brown sugar
½   cup cider vinegar
      Salt and pepper to taste

Combine the shallots, margarine, and sugar in a heavy skillet over medium heat and cook and stir until the butter and sugar have melted, about 5 minutes. Reduce the heat to low and simmer for 15 minutes, stirring frequently so that the shallots don't stick. Add the vinegar, salt, and pepper, and simmer until the mixture thickens, about 20 minutes. Cool and store in airtight jars in the refrigerator. The jam will keep for several weeks in the refrigerator. Make sure there's a half-inch head space in the jars or containers if you plan to freeze them for longer storage.

Preparation time: 15 minutes
Cooking time: 40 minutes
Yield: About 2 cups

Onion Tarts

Pack onion tarts in a lunch box or picnic basket. Serve them as a hot or cold first course. They're so easy to make, it's guaranteed they'll make regular appearances at the dining table.

1	single-crust pie pastry, homemade or commercial
1	tablespoon olive oil
2	large onions, thinly sliced
3	large eggs
¼	cup low-fat or skim milk
	Pepper to taste
2	tablespoons chopped chives
½	teaspoon ground mace
1	teaspoon dried mustard

Preheat the oven to 350° F. Lightly oil 12 shallow muffin cups or a special tartlet tin tray.

Roll out the pastry into a ⅛-inch-thick rectangle. Using a 3-inch-round pastry cutter, cut out 12 circles and fit into the tartlet tins. Pat the pastry up the sides and around the rims of the molds and press down with fork tines. Chill in the refrigerator. Heat the oil in a skillet over medium heat and sauté the onions for 5 minutes. Remove the onions from the skillet and allow to cool. In a small bowl, beat together the eggs and milk. Stir in the pepper, chives, mace, and mustard. Spoon the onion into the tart shells and pour the egg mixture over the top. Bake on the top shelf of the oven for 15 to 20 minutes, until a knife inserted in the center comes out clean. Serve hot, or cool on a wire rack.

Preparation time: 25 minutes
Cooking time: 20 minutes
Yield: 12 tarts

Pie Crust

1½	cups presifted all-purpose flour
1	stick sweet butter or margarine, sliced in tablespoons
1	teaspoon lemon juice or vinegar
3	to 4 tablespoons ice water

Measure the flour into a medium-size bowl. Add the butter and cut into crumbs with a pastry blender or 2 knives (or use a food processor and pulse). Using a fork, stir in the lemon juice and water, 1 tablespoon at a time (or add to the food processor gradually while pulsing). Once you can shape the mixture into a ball, remove from the bowl, flatten, and wrap in waxed paper. Refrigerate for 20 minutes.

On a floured surface, roll out the pastry into a circle large enough to hang at least ½ inch over the edge of the pie dish. Press into a lightly greased pie dish and turn under the excess pastry. Pinch and flute the edges. Refrigerate until ready to use. To bake an unfilled pie shell, prick the bottom and sides of the pastry with a fork to allow air to escape during baking. Bake in a preheated 450° F oven 5 to 10 minutes for a pre-baked shell. For a fully baked shell, line the inside of the pastry with aluminum foil, fill with dried beans, and bake for 20 minutes in a 425° F oven.

Pearl Onion Chutney

This dish makes an attractive addition to a table of festive holiday foods.

10	small pearl onions
1	tablespoon olive oil
1	medium yellow onion, chopped (¾ cup)
2	cloves garlic, minced
1	pound canned whole peeled tomatoes, chopped
½	cup golden raisins
¾	cup cider vinegar
¼	cup brown sugar
1	teaspoon ground ginger
¼	teaspoon ground cloves
½	teaspoon ground nutmeg
	Salt and pepper to taste

Cut a cross on the bottoms of the onions and blanch 60 seconds in boiling water. Remove the skin carefully so that the base is left intact and the onions are left whole. Heat the oil in a 3-quart heavy stainless steel saucepan and sauté the chopped onion over medium heat for 3 minutes. Add the garlic and sauté for 2 minutes. Add the rest of the ingredients and simmer on low, uncovered, until the sauce has thickened and the onions are tender, about 40 minutes. Cool and spoon into a serving bowl.

Preparation time: 10 minutes
Cooking time: 45 minutes
Yield: 2½ cups

Even strong onions develop a sweetness when cooked. They add impact to such dishes as Onion Tarts (right), Pearl Onion Chutney, and Onion and Potato Gratin.

PARSNIPS

PASTINACA SATIVA, FAMILY UMBELLIFERAE

A native of Europe, the parsnip has been cultivated since Roman times. When the long, tapering root is left in the ground during the winter, frosty weather turns the starch content into sugar, and the cream-colored, crisp flesh develops a very sweet and nutty flavor. Although parsnips are a slow-growing crop, they can be harvested throughout the winter (as long as the ground is not frozen solid), when there is little else available in the home garden.

Commonly chopped up with carrots, or simply relegated to the soup pot, parsnips can take the spotlight in a stir-fry and also stand alone. Roasted in a little olive oil or butter, they are as succulent and as moist as sweet potatoes. In fact, before potatoes were introduced into Europe in the sixteenth century, parsnips were the major starch vegetable.

Two other roots, salsify and scorzonera, resemble parsnips, and can be used the same way.

Sweet and nutty-flavored parsnips are a good source of protein.

NUTRITIONAL VALUE

Like corn and potatoes, parsnips are very high in complex carbohydrate starches. A good source of vitamin C, magnesium, phosphorous, calcium, and folacin, parsnips are also high in potassium.

BUYING AND STORING

Available year-round, the parsnip actually has its peak season during the colder months. Choose those that are smooth and firm, without brown blemishes. Store them in a plastic bag in the refrigerator for up to 4 weeks. Homegrown parsnips can be left in the ground until April or harvested in the fall and stored in a root cellar for 4 months at temperatures not above 40° F. They must be kept moist in sand or in a room with little air circulation.

PREPARATION

Thin, young parsnips may need only a little scrubbing and are excellent for steaming or stir-frying. These are best shredded and thrown into a salad or, if they are very crisp, sliced into thin sticks and served with a dip. Larger, more mature parsnips harvested in late autumn or during the winter will need a thin layer of skin removed with a potato peeler. If the texture is soft, use them in soups or stews. Steamed or boiled, they are delicious when mashed with a little butter, pepper, nutmeg, and chopped parsley or chives. Another way to enhance their sweet flavor is to dip slices in flour, egg, and fine bread crumbs, and then sauté or deep-fry them.

Parsnip and Carrot Salad

3   *large carrots, peeled and shredded (about 2¼ cups)*
1   *large parsnip, peeled and shredded (about 1 cup)*
1   *medium zucchini, washed and shredded (about 1 cup)*
2   *Granny Smith apples, washed and shredded (about 2 cups)*
2   *tablespoons chopped fresh mint*
½   *cup Classic or Low-Fat Vinaigrette (page 115) made with rice or balsamic vinegar*

Place all shredded ingredients in a serving bowl. Sprinkle with the chopped mint and toss with the vinaigrette. Serve chilled or at room temperature.

Note: Grating the vegetables in a food processor shreds the flesh into longer pieces. The raw parsnips and carrots are a sweet mixture and team beautifully with sliced bananas, raisins, and shredded coconut. For such a combination, toss with vanilla or lemon yogurt, or mayonnaise flavored with honey and curry.

Preparation time: 20 minutes
Yield: 6 servings

Parsnip Crisp

Serve parsnip crisp as a light main meal or a hearty side dish.

2   *large potatoes, peeled and sliced ¼ inch thick*
3   *large parsnips, peeled and sliced ¼ inch thick*
1   *large onion, chopped*
1   *cup grated Parmesan cheese*
⅓   *cup chopped parsley Salt and pepper to taste*
1¼   *cups low-fat milk*
½   *teaspoon ground nutmeg*
1   *cup fresh bread crumbs*

Preheat the oven to 350° F and lightly oil an 8 × 10-inch baking dish.

Layer the potatoes, parsnips, and onion, sprinkling each layer with the grated Parmesan, parsley, salt, and pepper. Combine the milk and nutmeg and pour over the dish. The milk should not cover the vegetables. Sprinkle the top with the bread crumbs and remaining Parmesan cheese. Bake for 50 minutes, until the top is golden and the potatoes are tender.

Preparation time: 20 minutes
Cooking time: 50 minutes
Yield: 4 to 6 servings

Parsnip Fritters

4   parsnips, peeled and sliced (about 3½ cups)
2   tablespoons all-purpose flour
2   tablespoons finely chopped parsley
2   tablespoons finely chopped marjoram or oregano
¼   cup finely sliced scallions
1   egg, beaten
    Salt and pepper to taste
2   tablespoons all-purpose flour for coating
4   teaspoons vegetable oil

Cook the parsnips in boiling water in a covered saucepan or in the microwave for 10 to 15 minutes. Drain and mash. Sprinkle the flour over the top and stir in with the parsley, marjoram, scallions, egg, and seasonings. Form into small patties about ½ inch thick and roll in flour to give a light coating. Heat the oil in a large skillet over medium heat. Place the patties in the skillet and cook for 3 to 4 minutes. Turn and cook the second side for another 3 to 4 minutes, until golden brown. Serve immediately or keep warm in a very low oven.

Note: You can substitute black scorzonera or the long white roots of salsify in recipes calling for parsnips.

Preparation time: 20 minutes
Cooking time: 8 to 10 minutes
Yield: 4 servings

Parsnips are versatile vegetables that can be grated, sliced, or diced to add to many recipes. Use them raw in Parsnip and Carrot Salad, layer them with potatoes and onions and bake them in a Parsnip Crisp, or mash and mix them with herbs for delicious Parsnip Fritters.

PISUM SATIVUM, FAMILY LEGUMINOSAE

Peas have been eaten since the Bronze Age. Native to the eastern Mediterranean regions and northern Asia, peas were first cultivated in the Middle Ages and eaten as a dried vegetable or made into pea meal. Garden peas were developed by Italian gardeners during the sixteenth century, but it was not until the late seventeenth century that fresh peas became all the rage in France. The British aristocracy were quick to adopt this new continental craze, but pudding made from dried peas continued to be a staple food for the rest of the nation.

The pea deserves its place in history not only as the first vegetable to be canned and frozen, but also for being instrumental in the development of the science of genetics and hybridization.

There are three main types of peas: green peas (also called garden peas), with the inedible pod containing round or wrinkled (the sweeter of the two) peas; mangetout, with the edible pod (also called sugar snaps, Chinese peas, snow peas, and sugar peas); and petit pois, grown on dwarf varieties that produce small inedible pods containing tiny, sweet, and tender peas.

NUTRITIONAL VALUE
Peas are an excellent source of protein (1 cup offers 11 grams) and contain moderate amounts of calcium, phosphorus, potassium, folacin, and vitamins A and C.

BUYING AND STORING
Just like sweet corn, peas are full of sugar when they are young. Once picked, the sugar quickly turns to starch, so the best peas are those cooked within a day of harvesting. For the same rea-

Tender and sweet, garden fresh peas need to be cooked for only a few minutes.

son, frozen peas are more nutritious and sweeter than fresh peas that have been transported long distances or held in a store for several days.

Choose green shelling peas with smooth, firm, bright green pods about 3 inches long. The peas will be visible through the inedible pod, but they should be small and round rather than large, usually a sign of maturity. It's better to pick peas when young than to let them mature on the vines. Refrigerate in a plastic bag in the vegetable drawer for 2 days. For longer storage, shell them, blanch in boiling water for 1 minute, drop into a bowl of ice water, and drain. Freeze in airtight containers for up to 6 months.

PREPARATION

The best way to enjoy the full flavor of garden-fresh peas is to shell them just before using and cook in a covered pan with a little water for about 5 minutes—until heated through and tender. Another way is to sauté them in a little butter over very low heat for 5 to 10 minutes. Fresh (or flash-frozen) peas need no flavor enhancers except perhaps a small sprig of mint. Salt and pepper to taste after cooking.

Mangetout are at their best when small (depending on variety, the length of the pod will vary from 2 to 4 inches long) and the peas are not visible through the shell. Cut off the stem end and, if necessary, pull the string away and discard. Eat these peas raw in a salad or steam them for 3 to 5 minutes. Add to stir-fries for the last 2 to 3 minutes.

Sugar Pea and Lettuce Soup

When fresh local lettuce and peas are in seasonal abundance, make them into a flavorful light soup. This freezes well, so if your garden is producing more lettuce (or spinach) than you can serve up in salads, cook up several batches.

2 tablespoons olive oil
8 shallots, chopped small (about 1 cup)
2 cloves garlic, finely minced
½ cup chopped parsley
3 quarts vegetable stock or water with vegetable bouillon cubes
2 pounds small edible-pod peas, stem and string removed and cut in half
2 heads of loose-leaf or cos (romaine) lettuce, finely shredded
2 tablespoons chopped lovage or celery leaves
　Salt and pepper to taste
2 tablespoons chopped pineapple-sage leaves

Heat the oil in a 5-quart soup pot over medium heat. Add the shallots and sauté for 5 minutes until soft and slightly golden. Stir in the garlic and parsley and sauté for 2 minutes longer. Pour in the vegetable stock, turn the heat to high, and bring to a boil. Reduce the heat to medium-low, add the peas, lettuce, lovage, salt, and pepper. Cover the pot and simmer for 5 minutes, until the peas are tender and the lettuce has wilted. Stir in the pineapple-sage leaves. Pour the soup into a tureen and garnish with seasonal edible flowers like violet, viola, sage, sweet woodruff, or common thyme.

Preparation time: 20 minutes
Cooking time: 15 minutes
Yield: 12 servings

Peas and Onions

The classic French version of this dish is made with the white part of scallions.

2 tablespoons margarine or butter
12 scallions, white part only, cut in 1-inch pieces
¼ cup water
1 small head of Boston lettuce, cut in 8 wedges
3 cups fresh or frozen garden peas
　Salt and pepper to taste
⅓ to ½ cup low-fat sour cream
1 tablespoon chopped spearmint

Heat the margarine in a large skillet over low heat. Add the scallions and sauté for 2 minutes. Add the water and lettuce, cover the skillet, and cook for 5 minutes. Add the peas, return the cover, and simmer for 5 minutes. Season with salt and pepper and stir in the sour cream. Sprinkle with the chopped mint and serve immediately.

Preparation time: 10 minutes
Cooking time: 10 minutes
Yield: 4 to 6 servings

Combine peas with other vegetables for a change of pace, as in Sugar Pea and Lettuce Soup (opposite page) or Peas and Onions.

First discovered in the West Indies by Columbus, peppers are native to the uppermost reaches of South and Central America. They were introduced to other parts of the world by way of the Portuguese and Spanish trade routes during the fifteenth and sixteenth centuries. Pepper cultivation flourished in Africa, India, China, Thailand, and Hungary, and although they redefined many regional cuisines, they still enjoy unparalleled success in their native Mexico, where around 200 varieties are grown.

Peppers are divided into two main types: sweet peppers and hot chile peppers, which contain capsaicin, a volatile oil. Present in the interior veins and to a lesser extent in the seeds, capsaicin determines the degree of hotness.

SWEET PEPPERS
CAPSICUM ANNUUM

Bell Pepper
Thick, crisp flesh is green before ripening to red, yellow, orange, purple, or brown, depending on variety. Red bell peppers tend to have the sweetest flavor. Bell peppers vary in size from approximately 4 to 6 inches long.

Banana Pepper
Also called *la jaune royale*, it is similar in shape and texture to the Italian pepper, but the color develops to a ripe yellow. The flavor is sweet and mild.

Cherry Pepper
Sweet and spicy flavor not to be confused with hot chile cherry peppers. Most frequently used for pickling.

Italian Pepper
Sometimes called *cubanelle*, these peppers grow to about 6 inches long and 2 inches wide. The thin skin, which is pale green when immature, ripens to a yellow-orange. Its flavor is mild at all stages.

Red and yellow peppers are particularly sweet and tender, making them ideal for eating raw in salads or with dips and spreads. Like green bell peppers, they are good for stuffing with grains, pasta, or meats. All can be sliced and chopped for adding to stir-fries, sauces, relishes, soups, and as a topping for pizzas.

Sweet or hot, peppers come in a dazzling array of glossy colors.

HOT CHILE PEPPERS
CAPSICUM FRUTESCENS

Anaheim
Also called California green, long green, chile verde, and chile Colorado when a ripe red. The Anaheim pepper grows to about 7 inches long and the flavor is mildly spicy. Use it for stuffing with cheese and/or beans for chili rellenos or for making into the red or green sauce served with Mexican food. Dice and use to give a little zip to omelettes, stir-fries, cornbreads, soups, and stuffings. Delicious when roasted. Called *chile de la tierra* or *chile pasados* when dried.

Cayenne
Narrow, sometimes twisted, 2- to 4-inch-long pepper picked green for eating fresh or cooking. Left to ripen a deep red for drying and grinding into cayenne pepper. This pepper is very hot and used in many Chinese, Indian, Korean, and Vietnamese dishes. Cook whole and remove when desired spiciness is reached.

Habanero
Also called Scotch bonnet, the habanero pepper is small, about the size of a cherry tomato, and is considered to be the hottest of all the chile peppers. Harvested when dark green, pale yellow-green, and a ripe orange-red. Find it in ethnic specialty stores that sell Caribbean foods. Use raw or cooked with extreme care.

Hungarian Hot Wax
Sometimes called Armenian wax and hot Portugal, the Hungarian hot wax pepper grows 5 to 8 inches long and is robustly hot without destroying taste buds. This pepper and a milder wax variety are dried in Hungary and ground into sweet and hot paprikas. Good for pickling and relishes.

Jalapeño
Harvested when about 2 inches long and a deep green color. The flavor is intensely hot, especially when served with the seeds intact. A favorite for pickling and seasoning salsas and fillings for enchiladas and tacos. Slice raw to add impact to salads or a medley of fast stir-fried vegetables. *Chipotles*, the name for ripened and smoked jalapeños, are available dried and canned. For freezing purposes, roast or blanch whole.

Poblano
The poblano pepper is a mildly hot pepper with dark green, tough skin. It grows about 4 inches long and is somewhat heart-shaped. When roasted and skinned, it makes an ideal pepper for stuffing as chile rellenos. It's a good pepper for freezing raw or roasting unpeeled. Called *ancho* when ripened and dried, it can be reconstituted in water, pureed, and made into a piquant *mole* sauce. A hotter variety of poblano, also called *mulato* and *chilaca*, is sold as pasilla when dried.

Serrano
The Serrano pepper is lighter in color, a little longer, and sometimes even more twisted than the cayenne pepper. It is also hotter. To control spiciness in a cooked dish, add one whole serrano during cooking time and remove at the end. For a hotter flavor, slit the serrano and allow the oil from the interior veins (ribs) to seep into the sauce or soup. For immediate impact, add a minuscule amount of fresh, chopped serrano to salad dressings, salsas, and other dishes.

Thai
Also called red chile. Harvested when 1 inch long and green, and sometimes when a ripe red and about 2 inches long. The Thai pepper is very thin and super hot. Sometimes cut in half on a diagonal with the seeds left intact or shredded and tossed with seafood salads, this chile gives a mighty wallop to Thai dishes.

NUTRITIONAL VALUE
All peppers are an exceptional source of potassium and vitamins A and C, with the reddest and the hottest containing the most. One medium-size bell pepper contains more vitamin C than a large orange.

BUYING AND STORING
Hot and sweet peppers are available year-round in both fresh and dried forms. When buying fresh peppers, select those with firm, unblemished skin. If not using immediately, store in a plastic or paper bag in the vegetable bin of the refrigerator for up to 1 week. Purple and brown bell peppers are usually available from local sources during the summer months.

PREPARATION

Capsaicin, the volatile oil that is released when chile peppers are cut open, causes skin and eye irritation on contact. To avoid this problem, wear thin rubber gloves when slicing peppers open and removing seeds. To render a chile much milder, remove the inner ribs, where the major concentration of capsaicin is located. Rinse in cold water—hot water releases the fumes.

To enjoy the tender flesh and make peppers more digestible, the protective skin should be removed. Roasting under the broiler is one of the fastest and easiest methods. Broil peppers 3 inches from the heat, turning with tongs until the skins are evenly blistered on all sides. This may take 10 to 15 minutes. Remove from the heat and place in a paper bag or damp kitchen towel until cool enough to handle. Lay the peppers on a flat surface, loosen the skin at the stem end and pull down with the aid of a sharp paring knife. Cut off the stem, slit open, and remove the seeds and ribs.

When a chile pepper recipe sets a fire in your mouth, don't try to put it out with water or cold beer. Try these solutions instead: eat a spoonful of sugar or honey, or a dish of sorbet or ice cream; drink a glass of milk or yogurt.

Black Bean and Pepper Chili

Serve this spicy vegetarian chili over rice, bulghur, or quinoa, and you'll have a complete-protein dinner.

2   *tablespoons olive oil*
8   *to **10** cloves garlic, finely minced*
1   *fresh poblano pepper, chopped or crumbled*
1   *teaspoon (or to taste) fresh chopped cayenne pepper (or ½ teaspoon crushed dried)*
1   *large sweet pepper, chopped (about 1 cup)*
2   *large onions, chopped (about 2 cups)*
2   *large carrots, chopped (about 1½ cups)*
1   *rib celery, chopped (about ¾ cup), or 2 tablespoons fresh chopped lovage*
2   *pounds ripe tomatoes, pureed in blender or food processor (about 3 cups pureed)*
6   *cups cooked black beans*
1   *tablespoon ground coriander*
1   *tablespoon ground cumin*
1   *tablespoon dried oregano or **2** tablespoons chopped fresh oregano*
1   *cup low-fat sour cream*
6   *fresh or pickled jalapeño peppers, thinly sliced*

Heat the olive oil in a large saucepan or heavy pot and add the garlic, peppers, onions, carrots, and celery (or lovage). Stir and sauté over medium-high heat for 10 minutes. Stir in the pureed tomatoes, cooked beans, and seasonings. Lower the heat and simmer the chili for 20 minutes. Serve the chili on rice and garnish with sour cream and sliced jalapeños.

Preparation time: 30 minutes
Cooking time: 30 minutes (If using dried beans, add 1 hour.)
Yield: 6 to 8 servings

Couscous with Sweet and Hot Peppers

This bland cereal is a perfect vehicle for holding together a variety of textures and flavors. Experiment with different hot peppers for a spicier dish. To achieve a colorful effect when using green bell peppers, also use red chile peppers.

2   *tablespoons olive oil*
1   *medium red or Spanish onion, chopped (about ¾ cup)*
1   *large red or green sweet bell pepper, chopped small (about 1 cup)*
1   *to **2** tablespoons chopped fresh hot Hungarian wax or cayenne pepper*
2   *to **3** cloves garlic, finely minced*
2   *cups water or vegetable stock*
2   *cups couscous*
     Salt and pepper to taste
⅓   *cup chopped parsley*
1   *tablespoon chopped fresh cilantro or tarragon*
     Sprig cilantro for garnish

Heat 1 tablespoon of olive oil in a large skillet over medium heat and sauté the onion, peppers, and garlic for 3 minutes. Add the water. Turn up the heat to high and bring the water to a boil. Stir in the couscous, cover the skillet, and turn off the heat. After 5 to 10 minutes, season with salt and pepper. Stir in the remaining tablespoon of oil, parsley, and cilantro. Garnish with sprig of cilantro or parsley. Serve hot or cold as a main meal or side dish.

Preparation time: 15 minutes
Cooking time: 10 minutes
Yield: 8 servings

Stuffed Bell Peppers

This dish is both delicious and easy to prepare. For greater visual appeal, use a mixture of red, yellow, and green sweet peppers.

6   *large sweet peppers*
6   *ounces (1½ cups dry) elbow macaroni*
1   *tablespoon olive oil*
6   *scallions, thinly sliced (about 1 cup)*
1   *clove garlic, finely minced*
1   *cup grated part-skim mozzarella cheese*
1   *cup part-skim ricotta cheese*
¾   *cup grated reduced-fat cheddar cheese*
     Salt and pepper to taste
1   *teaspoon ground mace*
     Paprika to taste

Slice the stem caps off the peppers and reserve. Remove the seeds and membranes. Bring a pot of water to a boil and cook the peppers (and tops) for 5 minutes. Remove the peppers with a slotted spoon (reserve the water) and drain upside down. Bring the water back to a boil and cook the pasta for 6 minutes, until *al dente*. Drain off the water. Preheat the oven to 350° F and lightly oil a small, shallow baking dish. Heat the olive oil in a skillet over medium heat and sauté the scallions and garlic for 2 minutes. Spoon into a mixing bowl and add the drained pasta. Stir in the mozzarella, ricotta, and ½ cup of the

Ready in just 15 minutes, Couscous with Sweet and Hot Peppers is ideal for a fast family meal. Prepared ahead and chilled, it becomes weekend lunch, a picnic dish, or the perfect contribution to a potluck supper.

cheddar cheese. Season with the salt, pepper, and mace. Spoon in the prepared peppers. Place the peppers in the baking dish, sprinkle with the remaining ¼ cup of grated cheddar, and sprinkle with paprika. Cover the dish loosely with aluminum foil and bake on the middle shelf for 25 minutes. Remove the foil and the pepper caps and continue baking for 10 minutes, until golden brown and bubbly. Sprinkle a little more paprika over the top and decorate with the stem caps.

Preparation time: 20 minutes
Cooking time: 45 minutes
Yield: 6 servings

POTATOES

SOLANUM TUBEROSUM, FAMILY SOLANACEAE

The only buried treasure the Spanish explorers unearthed in South America came in the odd shapes of the many varieties of potatoes being grown in the Peruvian mountains by the Incas. Cultivated for more than 3,000 years by other Andean Indians, the *papa* became a staple of the Inca civilization. The Conquistadors took potato tubers back to Europe in the sixteenth century. There, it was rejected as being a poisonous member of the botanical family Solanaceae, which includes such deadly narcotics as mandrake and nightshade. Like its cousin the tomato, it took almost a century for the potato to be accepted as edible but, once embraced, its culture spread quickly throughout Europe. Europeans brought it back to the New World when they settled in North America in the seventeenth century. Back in Ireland, the potato had become such a staple that when a blight hit the crop in 1846, famine ravaged the country.

Today, potatoes are considered one of the world's staple crops, and several varieties are grown in 130 countries. According to appearance or color, they are divided into four main groups: round white, russet, round red, and long white. Within these groups are several varieties. Specialty groups include the yellow potatoes Yukon gold, Finnish, and fingerlings—potatoes with yellow skin and buttery-tasting, yellow flesh—and purple potatoes, with purple skin and flesh.

No one needs a lesson on how to cook potatoes, the starchy favorite of millions. However, there are enough classic and new recipes to let the cook create a different dish for every day of the year!

NUTRITIONAL VALUE

One large baked potato provides 4.65 g protein, 20 mg calcium, 115 mg magnesium, 844 mg potassium, 22 mcg folacin, 2.75 mg iron, and 26 mg vitamin C. When cooked in the microwave, it retains slightly more nutrients.

BUYING AND STORING

Two potatoes that everybody knows are new (early) potatoes and russet (Idaho) baking potatoes. New potatoes are excellent for boiling and serving with butter; their low starch, high moisture, and waxy texture also make them ideal salad potatoes. Freshly dug round whites or round reds are available as new potatoes in spring and autumn.

All-purpose round whites are not as waxy as reds and can be used for baking, mashing, french frying, and simmering in soups. In some varieties, the light brown skin is sometimes rough, but the flesh is usually moist and holds its shape. Red varieties have smooth, thin skin and because the creamy, waxy, and very moist flesh holds its shape, they are suitable for home fries, boiling, casseroles, gratins, and salads.

Russets are large, oval potatoes with thick, brown skin. The high-starch flesh is dry and mealy, ideal for making into fluffy baked potatoes and also good for thickening soups. Russets are available year-round. Long whites are about the same size as russets, but their skin is thin, smooth, and golden. The flesh is low in starch, very moist, and keeps its shape well. This potato is excellent for boiling, for making into french and home fries, and for using in potato salads.

Yellow potatoes are becoming more available in supermarkets and especially at farmers' markets. Low in starch, the flesh has a creamy, waxy texture. Depending on variety, the shape and size range from small and round to small and fingerlike to large and round. Yellow potatoes are quite delicious all-purpose potatoes.

PREPARATION

Scrub new potatoes or rub the skin off between the fingers. Boil with a sprig of fresh mint for approximately 30 minutes until tender but still firm. To cook in the microwave: arrange 10 2-inch-diameter potatoes in a single layer in a glass pie plate. Add 1 tablespoon water, cover tightly with plastic wrap and microwave on high for 10 minutes. Allow to stand for 3 minutes or so.

Potatoes boiled with the skins intact retain more nutrients than those that are peeled. However, remove eyes and any green discoloration, which is mildly toxic and can cause stomach upset. Also, it's easier to make mashed potatoes without skins, unless the skins are very thin and can be mashed right in with the flesh.

When adding milk to mashed potatoes, heat the milk first. Cold milk makes a denser mash. Also, when mashing, use a potato masher, ricer, fork, or electric mixer. These devices incorporate air into the mashed potatoes. When pureed in the food processor, low-starch potatoes turn into a solid, gummy mass.

When making potato salad, cook the potatoes in the skins to keep a firm shape. Thin skins can be left on, or peeled when the potatoes are cool enough to handle. Add a vinaigrette dressing to warm potatoes, since they will absorb more of the flavors.

Potatoes baked in tinfoil or wrapped after baking develop soft, moist skins from the trapped steam. When baking whole potatoes, prick their skins to allow the steam to escape, so they won't explode. A metal skewer inserted through the center of a potato helps it to bake faster.

Herbed Baked Potatoes

Tired of eating plain baked potatoes? For a real treat (and a surprise), let them bake with flavor packed inside.

4   *large round potatoes, scrubbed*
8   *teaspoons margarine or butter*
4   *teaspoons chopped chives*
4   *teaspoons chopped parsley*
1   *cup low-fat cottage cheese, pureed*
1   *tablespoon lemon juice, or to taste*
¼   *cup fresh chopped herbs (parsley, chives, tarragon, dill, etc.)*

Using an apple corer, carefully remove a plug from each potato without going through the bottom skin. Cut off the lower two thirds of the plug and discard. Fill each hole with 1 teaspoon each of margarine, chives, and parsley. Seal with 1 more teaspoon of margarine and the remaining top portion of the plug. Bake for 50 minutes at 400° F, until tender. Combine the cottage cheese, lemon juice, and herbs in a small serving bowl. Serve for spooning over the baked potatoes.

Preparation time: 20 minutes
Cooking time: 50 minutes
Yield: 4 servings

Hot Potato Salad

If you can find them, choose yellow potatoes for both texture and flavor; otherwise, use small round white or red potatoes for this salad.

4   *pounds thin-skinned potatoes, cut into 1-inch chunks*
⅔   *cup olive or vegetable oil*
⅓   *cup rice-wine vinegar*
    Salt and pepper to taste
4   *cloves garlic, crushed*
1   *tablespoon prepared mustard*
¼   *cup chopped fresh dill*
1   *medium-size onion, cut in half and thinly sliced*
8   *ounces goat or feta cheese, cut in bite-size pieces*

Place potatoes in a large saucepan, cover with water and the pan lid. Bring to a boil over high heat, reduce the heat to medium, and cook for 15 minutes, until the potatoes are tender. Drain. While potatoes are cooking, combine the oil, vinegar, salt, pepper, garlic, mustard, and dill in a small bowl. Add the onion and cheese. Pour this mixture over the drained, hot potatoes and stir with a rubber spatula to distribute the dressing. Turn into a serving bowl and leave at room temperature.

Preparation time: 20 minutes
Cooking time: 15 minutes
Yield: 8 to 10 servings

Roasted Garlic and Rosemary Potatoes

This is an easy way to cook "home-fried" potatoes for a crowd.

¼ cup olive oil
½ cup fresh chopped rosemary leaves or **3** tablespoons dried
8 cloves garlic, finely minced
   Salt and pepper to taste
10 large white or red potatoes, scrubbed and cut in ½-inch-thick slices

Preheat the oven to 400° F.

Combine the oil, rosemary, garlic, salt, and pepper in a large bowl. Add the potato slices and turn them until thoroughly coated with the dressing. Arrange in a large, shallow baking dish, slightly overlapping each slice. Place in the oven and bake for 60 minutes, until golden crisp.

Preparation time: 10 minutes
Cooking time: 60 minutes
Yield: 8 servings

Roasted Garlic and Rosemary Potatoes is just one of many flavorful and filling potato-based dishes.

 # PUMPKINS

CUCURBITA, FAMILY CUCURBITACEAE

At about the time the American Indians were showing the settlers how to plant and use pumpkins, New World explorers were introducing the genus *Cucurbita* (including pumpkins, summer and winter squashes, melons, cucumbers, and various other gourds) into Europe. Although the French enthusiastically made the large orange *citrouille* into jams, soups, puddings, and a variety of savory dishes, the pumpkin had little overall effect on European gastronomy. The American colonists, on the other hand, relied on pumpkins as a winter staple and were more resourceful and imaginative, making them into butter, sauces, syrups, soups, puddings, pies, and a variety of breads.

America continues its love affair with the pumpkin and each year more than 40 million pounds are purchased. Large pumpkins, jack-o'-lantern and Connecticut field varieties, are most commonly used for carving. Even though they can be used for baking, pie fillings, and custard-type dishes, the smaller sugar varieties, such as New England pie, are far superior.

The difference between pumpkins and winter squash is confusing. For example, the great big max pumpkins, which weigh more than 100 pounds, are of the *Cucurbita maxima* species, just like the buttercup and hubbard squashes. The species *Cucurbita moschata* includes Kentucky field pumpkins, a number of other pumpkins, and butternut squash. *Cucurbita pepo* is perhaps the most confusing. This species includes Connecticut field and jack-o'-lantern pumpkins, winter squashes like acorn and vegetable spaghetti, and also the summer squashes zucchini and yellow crookneck.

NUTRITIONAL VALUE
Pumpkin flesh is high in beta-carotene (pro-vitamin A) and potassium. (Note that ½ cup home-cooked pumpkin contains 1,320 IU of vitamin A.) Pumpkin flesh also offers moderate amounts of calcium and phosphorus, and small amounts of vitamin C and magnesium. Pumpkin flowers and leaves are also high sources of vitamin A, while leaves rival spinach in iron content.

BUYING AND STORING
Pumpkins are available from October into the winter months. Be sure to choose firm, smooth pumpkins with unbroken and unblemished skin that are heavy for their size.

When buying pumpkins for dessert recipes, select small sugar pumpkins weighing from 3 to 10 pounds. These pumpkins have been specially developed for eating purposes and have a higher sugar content than the larger field pumpkins. Field pumpkins have a high moisture content; the flesh tends to be stringy and does not make a smooth puree. They are not good for making into pie filling, but they are fine for cubing to add to soups and stews. You can also peel, steam, and mash them for use in breads and muffins.

If sugar pumpkins are not available, choose small field or cushaw pumpkins, or butternut or red hubbard squash. They have firm flesh and a good, sweet flavor, and make a thick puree.

For short-term storage, place in the refrigerator for 2 weeks. Longer refrigeration spoils the flavor and texture.

Warm temperatures cause squash to wrinkle, dry out, or rot. To keep for 2 to 3 months, store in a dry, ventilated environment at 50 to 55° F.

PREPARATION

Pumpkins can be steamed, boiled, or baked. Cut in half with a sharp kitchen knife. Scoop out the seeds and cut into quarters, then halve the quarters. Place the pieces in a large saucepan and add 2 inches of boiling water. Cover and cook on low heat for 25 minutes or until the flesh is tender. Drain and cool. Remove the rind from the pieces and puree the flesh. This puree is not as firm as that of baked pumpkin and may require draining when intended for pie or mousse. Puree can be frozen in airtight containers for up to a year.

To bake whole: place on a baking sheet and bake in a 350° F oven for 1 to 1½ hours for a pumpkin weighing 3 pounds. Cut in half and scoop out the seeds and fibers. (Seeds can be eaten raw, sprouted, or best of all, roasted.) Scrape the flesh from the skin and mash, puree in a food processor, or press through a food mill. One pound of pumpkin will give about 1 cup of cooked puree.

To cube raw pumpkin flesh, first cut in half and remove seeds, then cut into quarters and peel thinly. Cut into 1-inch-thick slices and then into 1-inch cubes.

Curried Vegetarian Pumpkin Stew

This is a true stick-to-your ribs stew of winter vegetables and lentils—full of protein, fiber, and flavor.

2	*tablespoons olive oil*
1	*large red onion, chopped (about 1¼ cups)*
4	*cloves garlic, crushed*
2	*teaspoons ground cumin*
2	*teaspoons ground coriander*
2	*teaspoons ground turmeric*
1	*to **2** tablespoons curry paste*
2	*large carrots, sliced ¼ inch thick (about 2 cups)*
1	*pound can roughly chopped (chunked), stewed tomatoes (2 cups)*
1½	*cups vegetable stock*
4	*ounces lentils (½ cup)*
1	*pound pumpkin, peeled, seeded, and cut into 1-inch cubes*
1	*cup nonfat plain yogurt*
½	*cup chopped cilantro or chives*
½	*cup fresh sliced red hot chiles*

Heat the oil in a 4- to 5-quart heavy saucepan and cook the onion, garlic, cumin, coriander, and turmeric for 5 minutes over medium heat. Stir in the curry paste and carrots and cook 5 minutes over a low heat. Stir in the tomatoes, stock, and lentils and bring to a boil over medium-high heat. Reduce the heat to low, cover the pot, and simmer for 10 minutes. Add the pumpkin and cook for 15 to 20 minutes, until tender. To serve, spoon into individual soup dishes and top with 2 tablespoons yogurt and 1 teaspoon chopped cilantro. Pass the rest of the yogurt, cilantro, and the hot chiles separately at the table.

Preparation time: 20 minutes
Cooking time: 35 minutes
Yield: 4 servings

Pumpkin-Cheese Soufflé

An impressive way to start off a meal, individual soufflés are easy to make—there's no flour sauce base involved, and they can be made ahead. Thirty minutes before dinner, preheat the oven, beat the egg whites, fold through, and bake.

1	*2-pound pumpkin, cut in half, seeds removed (2 cups puree)*
1	*cup cottage cheese*
3	*large eggs, separated*
½	*cup grated reduced-fat Cheddar cheese*
¼	*cup chopped chives or thinly sliced scallion greens*
1	*tablespoon chopped fennel leaves Salt and pepper to taste*

Place the pumpkin in a microwaveable container cut side down, cover with plastic wrap and microwave on high for 10 minutes. Or, place in a saucepan with 1 to 2 inches of water and steam for 20 minutes, until tender. Preheat the oven to 375° F and lightly butter 4 8-ounce soufflé dishes.

Remove the pulp from the pumpkin shell (about 2 cups) and place in a mixing bowl or food processor. Add the cottage cheese and egg yolks. Beat or process until smooth. Stir in the cheddar cheese, chives, fennel leaves, salt, and pepper. In a large metal or glass bowl, beat the egg whites until stiff. Stir one third of the whites into the squash mixture then fold in the rest. Spoon into the soufflé dishes and bake 25 minutes, until puffed and golden.

Note: You can substitute any winter squash for the pumpkin.

Preparation time: 20 minutes
Cooking time: 25 to 30 minutes
Yield: 4 servings.

Praline Pumpkin Pudding

Bake this pudding as a special dessert to end a dinner party. And don't wait for autumn to come around—it's just as good with canned pumpkin puree.

2	cups pumpkin puree
2	large eggs, separated
1	cup brown sugar
1	tablespoon ground cinnamon
1	teaspoon ground ginger
½	teaspoon ground nutmeg
¼	teaspoon ground cloves
1½	cups skim or regular evaporated milk

Preheat the oven to 350° F and lightly butter 6 individual glass baking dishes.

Combine all the ingredients, except the egg whites, in a large mixing bowl and beat together. In a large metal or glass mixing bowl, beat the egg whites until stiff, stir one third into the pumpkin mixture, and fold in the rest gently. Spoon into the baking dishes, place on a baking tray, and bake on the middle shelf of the oven for 25 minutes, until a knife inserted in the center comes out clean. Serve at room temperature or chilled topped with Praline Topping.

Preparation time: 10 minutes
Cooking time: 25 minutes
Yield: 6 servings

Praline Topping

¼	cup sweet butter
¼	cup brown sugar
½	cup chopped almonds
3	tablespoons slivered blanched almonds, toasted

In a small saucepan, melt butter and sugar and boil for 2 minutes. Add the chopped almonds, stir to coat with the melted butter. Allow to cool. Break up and crumble. Sprinkle 1 tablespoon over pudding and top with a few toasted slivered almonds.

Praline Pumpkin Pudding is a festive dessert that is easy to prepare. You can bake this pudding in one large dish for 45 minutes, until set.

A native of southwest Asia, this tender, dark green, leafy plant was cultivated more than 2,000 years ago by the Romans and Greeks. In 430 B.C. the Greek physician Hippocrates talked of its medicinal properties. Other records indicate that it was taken to China from Nepal in A.D. 647.

There are two types of spinach; one has smooth, flat leaves, while the other has deeply crumpled leaves. Many varieties of spinach will grow only in the cooler conditions of autumn through spring, although there are some varieties that will tolerate the warmer weather of early summer. In cooler European climes, spinach can be a year-round crop. New Zealand spinach, which grows well in hot, dry climates, is an unrelated look-alike belonging to the Azioaceae family. Another warm-weather substitute for true spinach is the climbing Malabar spinach (*Basella alba*), which has dark green, large, heart-shaped leaves.

NUTRITIONAL VALUE

Like other dark green, leafy vegetables, spinach is rich in minerals and vitamins. Just ½ cup of steamed fresh spinach provides almost 8,000 IU vitamin A, 8.9 mg vitamin C, 2.7 g protein, 122 mg calcium, and 419 mg potassium. Frozen spinach has lower values but is still a good bet.

BUYING AND STORING

A cool-weather vegetable, spinach is at its peak in spring and again in early autumn. Buy clean, bright green leaves—small ones for eating raw, larger ones for cooking. Use immediately in a salad or store in a plastic bag in the refrigerator vegetable drawer for 2 days.

PREPARATION

This is a low-growing crop and, if not mulched, picks up soil on both the lower and upper sides of the leaves. Crinkly spinach in particular may need rinsing in several changes of cold water.

It's a crime to cook tender, young spinach leaves. Their mild but distinctive flavor adds interest to a salad and is particularly good when combined with fresh, firm raw mushrooms. Large mature leaves are best served cooked. They can be wilted and chopped for stuffing into pastas, crepes, and omelettes; pureed and combined with eggs for soufflés and roulades; added to a stir-fry dish during the last minute; or simply steamed and served with butter and seasonings.

When steaming spinach, use only the water that clings to the leaves after washing—just lift from the final rinse and place in a saucepan. Cover tightly and cook over low heat for 5 minutes, until wilted.

Spinach Dumplings (Gnocchi)

These little dumplings are ready to toss with a sauce or cheese as soon as they come to the surface of the boiling water. However, they can also be spooned into a baking dish, refrigerated, and then baked later with a drizzle of olive oil and a sprinkle of Parmesan cheese or a few spoonfuls of fresh tomato sauce.

2 cups all-purpose flour
1½ cups low-fat ricotta cheese
¾ cup grated Parmesan cheese
1 large egg, beaten
1 teaspoon ground nutmeg
  Salt and pepper to taste
¼ cup chopped fresh chives
1 pound fresh spinach, steamed and chopped fine or **1** 10-ounce packet frozen spinach, thawed and drained of liquid
¼ cup all-purpose flour
2 to **4** tablespoons olive oil or melted butter
½ cup grated Parmesan cheese
2 cups Fresh Tomato Sauce (page 112)

Place the flour in a large mixing bowl, make a well in the middle, and add the ricotta, Parmesan cheese, beaten egg, nutmeg, salt, pepper, chives, and chopped spinach. Blend well together. Pinch the dough into 1-inch balls and roll lightly in the ¼ cup flour. Place on a tray so that the dumplings do not touch each other. Refrigerate until ready to use. Bring a pot of water to a boil and drop a few dumplings at a time into the boiling water. As the dumplings rise to the top, remove with a slotted spoon to a lightly oiled, shallow baking dish. Drizzle with oil or butter, sprinkle with the Parmesan cheese, and bake in a preheated 350° F oven for 15 minutes, until hot, or place 6 inches under the broiler and broil for 5 minutes until the cheese is golden brown. If desired, serve with Fresh Tomato Sauce (page 112).

Preparation time: 20 minutes
Cooking time: 15 to 25 minutes
Yield: 4 to 6 servings

Spinach-Stuffed Tomatoes

Besides tasting delicious, these stuffed tomatoes have great visual appeal.

4	*large or **8** medium tomatoes*
2	*tablespoons olive oil*
1	*medium onion, finely chopped (about ¾ cup)*
2	*cloves garlic, crushed or minced*
2	*pounds fresh spinach, steamed and chopped, or **2** 10-ounce packets frozen, chopped spinach, thawed and drained*
1	*cup dried bread crumbs*
1	*beaten egg*
	Salt and pepper to taste
1	*teaspoon dried thyme leaves*
1	*teaspoon dried oregano leaves*

Cut the tomatoes in half horizontally and scoop out the seeds and juice (about 1 tablespoonful). Place tomato halves in a lightly oiled baking dish. Heat the oil in a skillet over medium heat and sauté the onion 3 minutes. Add the garlic and sauté 2 minutes longer. Remove from the heat and stir in the spinach, bread crumbs, egg, salt, pepper, thyme, and oregano. Spoon the mixture into the hollowed tomato halves and bake in a 350° F oven for 25 to 30 minutes, until hot and golden.

Preparation time: 20 minutes
Cooking time: 30 minutes
Yield: 4 to 8 servings

Serve Spinach-Stuffed Tomatoes as a light supper or as a hearty side dish.

SQUASHES

CUCURBITA, FAMILY CUCURBITACAEA

Winter and summer squashes and pumpkins are all members of the same family. Cucurbits, as they are known, were first cultivated in Central America as early as 6,000 B.C. The name "squash" comes from the Native-American word *askutasquash*, meaning "eaten raw or uncooked." And while seventeenth-century European settlers were introduced to native squash varieties, or "vine apples of several colors" as Roger Williams, the founder of Rhode Island, referred to them, it's possible they had already tasted or heard of zucchini and pumpkin squashes in Europe. Seeds of both had been brought back by Italian and Spanish explorers during the sixteenth century.

Botanically, the squashes are a complicated lot to sort out. Fortunately, classification doesn't mean a thing when it comes to cooking with squash. All you need to know is which squashes are interchangeable in recipes.

WINTER SQUASHES

CUCURBITA PEPO, C. MAXIMA, AND C. MOSCHATA

Winter squashes have thick, tough skins, and the yellow or orange flesh is moist and flavorful. Protected by such hard shells, they can be stored to last through the winter months. With their ridges, dents, and lumps, winter squashes are an odd-shaped bunch. Some are very large; others are not much bigger than a baking potato. Large or small, and no matter how delicious they are when cooked, these are the ones to buy in autumn to decorate the front porch or harvest table.

There are also many exotic squashes available, like the West Indian pumpkin called *calabazas* or toadback; the Mexican *chayote*, also called *mirliton* and *choko*; *kabocha*, the generic name for Japanese winter squash; and the giant Tahitian squash.

The following are some old and new favorites:

Whereas the skins of acorn and butternut winter squashes are thick and hard, those of the summer squashes, such as the zucchini, are tender.

Acorn Squash

Also called "table queen" and "Des Moines" after the well-known varieties, acorn squash is a small, dark green acorn-shaped squash with deep vertical ridges. Yellow speckles on the skin are not as desirable as a solid green—unless it is one of the newer all-yellow varieties. The flesh is deep yellow to light orange, thick, and tender. Acorns weigh from 1 to 1½ pounds. This squash is usually cut in half, stuffed and baked, or cut into rings or wedges.

Butternut Squash

Bell-shaped, measuring from 7 to 9 inches long, butternuts weigh from 1 to 3 pounds. The smooth, thin, light brown skin is easy to peel. Fine-textured and smooth, the bright orange flesh has a sweet flavor. This squash is excellent for pies, cut in half and baked, cubed and sautéed, and steamed and pureed for soups.

Buttercup Squash

Weighing 2 to 4 pounds and with its distinctive knobby cap, the buttercup squash looks like a small Turk's turban squash. Its thick, dark green skin is striped with orange and the sweet, nutty-flavored orange flesh is smooth and fine textured. It makes an excellent all-purpose squash. Cook whole, halved, or in chunks. The large Turk's turban is just as delicious, and cooking methods are identical.

Golden Nugget Squash

A small, round, orange squash weighing 2 to 3 pounds, the golden nugget squash has thick, ridged skin when allowed to mature. When picked early, the skin is

much thinner. With its dense, nutty-flavored flesh, this squash is good when baked whole or halved, cut into chunks for soup, steamed, or sautéed. Other small pumpkin look-alikes include the deep orange Jack be-little and the creamy yellow sweet dumpling. Both are sweet and a perfect size for baking as single servings.

Hubbard Squash

There are blue, golden, gray, and green-warted hubbards, all large, long, and globular, with thick ridged or bumpy skin. They can weigh from 14 to 40 pounds. Hubbards have thick, fine-textured, yellow-orange flesh, and some varieties are dryer or sweeter. All-purpose squashes, they can be baked, steamed, cut in half or in chunks. Use those with dry-textured flesh for making pies. Large hubbards are sold by the piece.

Spaghetti Squash

The spaghetti squash is a broad, oblong, yellow-skinned squash weighing 1 to 3 pounds. The cream-colored flesh is unique in that when cooked, it can be separated with a fork into spaghetti-like strands. It was developed in Italy and improved by Japanese growers. The usual method of cooking is to bake or boil whole or halved. In the microwave, a 1-pound squash will cook in 10 minutes, and it should be turned over halfway through. Cut it in half, scoop out the seeds, and scrape out the flesh. Serve with a pasta sauce or toss with stir-fried vegetables.

NUTRITIONAL VALUE

Nutritional information is not available on all varieties. However, those with the deepest orange and the finest-textured flesh are the highest in vitamin A. For example, butternut squash is highest, with ½ cup baked cubes providing 7,141 IU vitamin A, 15.4 mg vitamin C, 290 mg potassium, and 42 mg calcium. The same amount of hubbard squash provides 6,156 IU vitamin A, 9.7 mg vitamin C, 365 mg potassium, and 17 mg calcium. The more fibrous acorn squash provides 437 IU vitamin A, 11 mg vitamin C, 446 mg potassium, and 45 mg calcium. Spaghetti squash provides 86 IU vitamin A, 2.7 mg vitamin C, 91 mg potassium, and 17 mg calcium. All are a moderate source of magnesium, phosphorus, and folacin.

BUYING AND STORING

Check for unblemished hard skins. Reject those with cracks or those that feel light or hollow. Those that feel heavy for their size will have dense, moist flesh. When buying cut pieces of the larger squashes, the flesh should be firm, moist, and a uniform bright color. Some winter squashes are now available year-round. However, newly harvested autumn squashes will be moister than those that are still coming out of storage at the beginning of the following summer.

PREPARATION

Most winter squashes are good stuffed and baked with butter and maple syrup, stuffed with apple slices and raisins, or baked and then garnished with bright green, tiny peas or ruby cranberry relish.

The thick-skinned, odd-shaped squashes are difficult to cut or peel. To cut in half, slice off the stem and, using a large, heavy kitchen knife, score the skin where it needs splitting. Insert the knife ¼ inch into the flesh close to the stem end and hit the knife blade where it meets the handle, gently, but firmly, with a hammer. Repeat until the squash splits open. Remove the seeds and place in a baking dish with 1 inch of water. Cover with foil and bake at 350° F for 30 to 60 minutes, depending on size. Check for doneness by pressing the skin, which will give when the flesh is tender.

When the flesh is destined for puree (for breads, muffins, soufflés, pies, and soups), avoid the hard cutting process by baking the lumpy squash whole. The skin will slice very easily once the flesh is tender. The smaller, smooth-skinned squashes are the easier ones to peel and cube when raw. Sauté or stir-fry cubes and slices in olive oil with garlic and onions. Toss into soups or serve as a vegetable side dish.

SUMMER SQUASHES

Summer squashes are of the same genus as most of the winter squashes, except they are not left to mature and grow hard skins. Rather, they are thin-skinned varieties that are at their best when picked young. At this stage, they are so tender they do not need peeling, and the seeds are almost unnoticeable. Young squashes have a firm and crunchy texture and are excellent for slicing and adding raw to a mixed salad or for marinating in a garlic-herb vinaigrette. Summer squashes are not as flavorful as the winter squashes.

Zucchini
Also called *cocozelle* and *courgette*, zucchini is probably the best known because it is so prolific in the garden. Most varieties are long, slender, and club-shaped with dark green skin. However, some hybrids are round, or a gray-green or even yellow color. Yellow zucchini is not to be confused with the yellow crookneck or straight-neck squashes.

Yellow Squashes
The "neck" squashes are commonly referred to as yellow or summer squashes. Colors vary from pale yellow to lemon to gold when young, deepening in intensity as they mature and toughen. The crookneck has an oblong shape that is swollen at the bottom and narrow and curved at the top. If left to mature, it can grow to at least 10 inches long. The straight-neck yellow squash resembles a skittle and can also grow to an immense length when not picked regularly. Depending on variety, the skin of these squashes is smooth or warty.

English Marrow Squash
The dark green and light-striped English marrow is a related squash that grows to quite a large size. (It looks like a giant zucchini, which also develops pale green stripes as it ages and can grow to more than 1 foot long by at least 3 inches in diameter.) Like zucchini, marrow squash has more flavor when picked young, but many people prize the large ones for hollowing out, stuffing

with a bread-and-onion dressing, and baking whole.

Scallop Squash

Scallop squash is a small, flattened, round squash with scalloped edges. It is also called patty pan, custard squash, and cymling. When very young the skin is light green, turning white as the squash matures. These are most tender when picked at 2 to 4 inches wide.

NUTRITIONAL VALUE

Like the winter squashes, the summer ones can be used to add nutrition to both savory dishes and sweet desserts. A half-cup of cooked zucchini provides 216 IU vitamin A, 15 mcg folacin, 4.2 mg vitamin C, 228 mg potassium, and 12 mg calcium. Yellow neck squashes provide 259 IU vitamin A, 18 mcg folacin, 5 mg vitamin C, 173 mg potassium, 24 mg calcium. Scallop squash provides 77 IU vitamin A, 18.6 mcg folacin, 9.7 mg vitamin C, 126 mg potassium, and 14 mg calcium.

BUYING AND STORING

Select small, young squashes with unblemished skin. The skin of fresh squash has a satinlike bloom and on smooth squash feels silky. Choose those that feel heavy and reject those with dull, wrinkled skin. The skin of large, mature squashes is thicker and, like scallop and neck varieties, will need peeling. The seeds are also much larger in older squashes and the flesh often has a wooly texture. Such squashes will be too light for their size.

Use as soon as possible to preserve the crunchy texture, or store in a plastic bag in the vegetable drawer of the refrigerator for up to 4 days. Because they do not store well, squash blossoms are best used the same day they're picked.

PREPARATION

Firm, young squashes need only to be washed and trimmed before they are sliced, diced, or julienned. They can then be used in quick-cooked pasta toppings or stir-fry dishes, or on a vegetable pizza.

Medium- and large-sized squashes may need peeling before they are grated for breads, muffins, pancakes, and cake recipes. Mature squashes can be sliced lengthwise or crosswise and pickled. They are also great for sautéeing, breading and frying, boiling, baking, and stuffing whole. Shredded or cubed, they can be made into soups.

To prepare squash blossoms: remove the stems and any greens attached, rinse, and blot dry very gently between paper towels. Open the blossoms and stuff with a variety of fillings: creamed cheese, egg and chive salad, or peas. Or stuff with a rice mixture and bake at 350° F for 15 to 20 minutes. Squash blossoms can also be dipped in a tempura batter and deep-fried.

Cream of Winter Squash Soup

Satisfying to make and eat, this spicy soup can be made very quickly.

2	*tablespoons olive oil or butter*
1	*large leek, washed, trimmed, and thinly sliced (about 2 cups)*
4	*large cloves garlic, minced or crushed*
2	*pounds winter squash (butternut, acorn, hubbard), peeled, seeded, and cut into 1-inch cubes (about 4 cups)*
2¾	*cups vegetable stock*
½	*teaspoon ground ginger*
½	*teaspoon ground nutmeg*
½	*teaspoon ground coriander Salt and pepper to taste*
¾	*cup buttermilk or half-and-half Parsley or cilantro leaves for garnish*

Heat the olive oil in a 4- to 5-quart kettle and sauté the leeks and garlic for 5 minutes over medium heat. Add the squash, stock, ginger, nutmeg, coriander, salt, and pepper. Cover the pot and bring to a boil. Reduce the heat to low and simmer for 25 minutes, until the squash is tender. Using a food processor or blender, process one third of the soup at a time. Return the soup to the pot, pour in the buttermilk, and reheat for 5 minutes. To serve, spoon into individual bowls and garnish with parsley or cilantro.

Preparation time: 15 minutes
Cooking time: 35 minutes
Yield: 4 servings

Cold Summer Squash Soup

Prepare this soup with any of the summer squashes—even overgrown ones that have not reached the pithy stage.

2	tablespoons olive oil
1	cup chopped shallots
2	cloves garlic, minced
3	cups grated squash, including skin if unblemished
2	tablespoons all-purpose flour
1½	cups vegetable stock or skim milk
½	cup nonfat plain yogurt
½	cup low-fat sour cream
1	tablespoon chopped fresh cilantro or tarragon
2	tablespoons chopped fresh chives
	Salt and pepper to taste

Heat the oil in a large skillet and sauté the shallots and garlic over medium heat for 3 minutes. Add the grated squash and sauté for 10 minutes. Stir in the flour and cook for 2 minutes. Add the vegetable stock, increase the heat to medium-high, and stir until the sauce thickens. Remove from the heat and spoon into a bowl. Stir in the yogurt, sour cream, cilantro, chives, salt, and pepper. Refrigerate and serve chilled.

Preparation time: 15 minutes
Cooking time: 25 minutes
Yield: 4 servings

Chocolate-Nut Zucchini Cake

This is a lovely, moist chocolate cake with a cream-cheese filling. Add 2 to 4 tablespoons cocoa to the filling for a richer flavor.

1	cup sugar
2	large eggs
½	cup sweet margarine or sweet butter, softened
1¼	cup all-purpose flour
½	cup cocoa (not Dutch)
1	tablespoon baking powder
½	teaspoon baking soda
½	cup milk
1	teaspoon vinegar
1¼	cups shredded zucchini
1	cup finely chopped walnuts

Frosting
8	ounces low-fat Neufchâtel cream cheese
½	cup low-fat sour cream
½	cup confectioners' sugar
1	tablespoon vanilla extract

Preheat the oven to 350° F and butter and flour two 9-inch-diameter cake pans.

Beat the sugar, eggs, and margarine together in a large mixing bowl with electric beaters until thick and fluffy. Combine the flour, cocoa, baking powder, and baking soda in a small bowl and sift into the egg mixture one third at a time, alternating with the milk. Gently stir in the vinegar, zucchini, and chopped walnuts. Spoon into the prepared pans and bake in the middle of the oven for 20 minutes, until a skewer inserted in the center comes out clean. Allow to cool in the pans for 5 to 10 minutes, then turn out onto a wire rack.

Beat together the cream cheese, sour cream, confectioners' sugar and vanilla extract. Spread one third of this mixture over one cake layer, cover with the second layer, and spread the rest of the frosting over the top and down the sides.

Preparation time: 20 minutes
Cooking time: 20 minutes
Yield: 12 slices

This chocolate Zucchini Cake (opposite page) looks terrific with vanilla frosting on top.

Cold Summer Squash Soup.

IPOMOEA BATATAS, FAMILY CONVOLVULACEAE

The sweet potato is native to Central and South America, where it was cultivated by the Aztecs, Incas, and Mayas. Spanish explorers also discovered Indians growing sweet potatoes in the West Indies and southern areas of North America. Transported to Europe during the sixteenth century, these sweet tubers were introduced by the Spanish under their South American Indian (and scientific) name, *batatas*, meaning "sweet potato." The name "potato" was also given to the unrelated white tubers of *Solanum tuberosum*, which were brought back from Peru some years later.

An important crop for colonists in the southern part of the United States, sweet potatoes were also a staple food for black slaves, who called the yellow-fleshed, chestnut-flavored tuber "yam" after their own African vegetable called *nyami*. Native to Africa and Asia, *nyami* is a rhizome and belongs to the family *Dioscoreacea*. African and Asian yams are large and may weigh from 7 to 40 pounds. Rough, brown skin encases the mildly sweet, light-colored flesh, which is used as a starch vegetable in West Indian, African, and Asian dishes.

The deep orange variety of yams is moister and sweeter than the pale yellow type.

There are three distinct types of sweet potatoes: white (no longer commercially popular), pale yellow, and reddish orange. Even today, the moist, dark orange-fleshed variety is erroneously referred to as "yam."

Like pumpkins, sweet potatoes can be used in savory and sweet dishes. Substitute mashed sweet potatoes in breads, pies, soufflés, and any other recipe calling for pureed pumpkin. Sliced or grated raw, sweet potato may be substituted for white potatoes in soups, stews, and griddle cakes.

NUTRITIONAL VALUE

One half-cup of baked, mashed sweet potato provides 21,822 IU of natural vitamin A, or beta-carotene. This small amount of sweet potato also contains 1.72 grams of protein, 28 mg of calcium, 348 mg of potassium, 24.6 mg of vitamin C, 22.6 mcg of folacin, and good amounts of magnesium and phosphorus. Clearly this is a potato worth eating several times a week!

BUYING AND STORING

Choose sweet potatoes with unblemished skins, and when planning to cook them whole, buy those of uniform size. Freshly dug, uncured potatoes are available from late summer into early autumn. This is when they have a higher moisture content, a richer flavor, and a smoother texture than those that come out of long-term storage. Fresh sweet potatoes start to decay about 4 weeks after harvest. To prolong shelf life, growers "cure" them for a week by removing some of the moisture content with high temperatures and humidity, a process that toughens the skin, increases sweetness, and slows down deterioration.

When cured, these potatoes will keep for 9 months if stored at 65° F and 95 percent humidity. They will last for about 2 weeks when stored at room temperatures of 55 to 60° F. When refrigerated, the skin hardens and they develop an unpleasant flavor. Store only cooked potatoes in the refrigerator for up to 1 week and in the freezer for 2 to 3 months.

PREPARATION

Scrub the potatoes and bake, boil, or steam with the skins on. Once cooked, the skins peel off in one piece. Bake in a 400° F oven for 35 to 45 minutes, depending on size. In the microwave, they take about 6 minutes per potato when cooked on high power. For mashing purposes, cut in half or thirds, and boil or steam for 25 to 30 minutes until tender. Remove the skins and mash with 2 to 4 tablespoons of sour cream or butter, salt and pepper to taste, and ⅛ teaspoon nutmeg.

Sweet Potato Pie

This pie is a welcome change to pumpkin pie. To make without a crust, lightly oil a 9-inch pie plate and dust with toasted chopped nuts or crumbled cookies.

1	single 9-inch pie crust
2	cups mashed sweet potato (from canned or fresh potatoes)
2	large eggs
¾	cup brown sugar
1⅓	cups evaporated skim milk
1	teaspoon ground cinnamon
½	teaspoon ground nutmeg
½	teaspoon ground ginger
2	tablespoons bourbon or rum

Preheat oven to 425° F. Roll out pastry and fit into a 9-inch pie plate. Refrigerate.

Beat together the rest of the ingredients in a large bowl. Pour into the chilled pie shell and place in the center of the oven. Bake at 425° F for 15 minutes. Reduce the heat to 375° F and continue baking for 35 minutes, until a knife inserted into the center comes out clean. Cool on a wire rack before serving.

Preparation time: 10 minutes for pie filling, 10 minutes for pastry
Cooking time: 50 minutes
Yield: 8 servings

Sweet Potato Nut Bread

1	large sweet potato, cooked and mashed (about 1 cup)
¼	cup vegetable oil
2	large eggs, separated
½	cup orange juice
1½	teaspoons finely grated orange rind
¾	cup brown sugar
2	cups presifted, all-purpose flour
1	tablespoon baking powder
½	teaspoon baking soda
1	teaspoon ground cinnamon
½	teaspoon ground nutmeg
½	teaspoon ground allspice
1	cup chopped blanched almonds
1	cup shredded coconut

Preheat the oven to 350° F and lightly oil a 9 × 5 × 4-inch loaf pan. Line with baking paper and lightly oil.

In a large mixing bowl, beat together the mashed sweet potato, oil, egg yolks, orange juice, orange rind, and brown sugar. In a medium mixing bowl, combine the flour, baking powder, baking soda, cinnamon, nutmeg, and allspice. Stir gently into the liquid mixture. Stir in the chopped almonds and ¾ cup shredded coconut. In a large glass or stainless steel bowl beat the egg whites until stiff peaks form. Stir one third of the beaten whites into the batter, then fold in the rest. Spoon into the prepared loaf pan, sprinkle with the remaining ¼ cup coconut, and bake in the middle of the oven for 65 minutes, until a skewer inserted in the center comes out clean.

Preparation time: 25 minutes
Cooking time: 65 minutes
Yield: 12 to 14 slices

Sweet Potato Nut Bread can be made with pale yellow sweet potatoes or with deep orange ones, which make it denser and moister.

LYCOPERSICON ESCULENTUM, FAMILY SOLANACEAE

Native to Mexico and Peru, the *tomati* was first cultivated by the Aztecs. Transported to Europe in the early sixteenth century, this vegetable was embraced by the Spaniards and Italians for its gastronomic value. This wasn't the case in the rest of Europe, where this relative of the poisonous Nightshade family was grown as a curiosity and a decorative plant bearing "golden apples." This term was not entirely incorrect—the tomato is actually a fruit or, in fact, a large berry. Although the French were eating the *pomme d'amour* around 1750, it was not until the mid-1800s that this "love apple" lost its sordid reputation as an aphrodisiac and a poison in England and America. Today, in the United States and some Mediterranean countries, it is the most important crop grown for canning purposes and the most revered vegetable for the home garden.

Tomatoes come in all shapes and sizes and vary in color from pale lemon to rich yellow, and from pale pink to the deepest red. Some are shaped like miniature pears, others are as small as cherries, and those of the beefsteak variety grow as big as grapefruit. The ones that are ripened on the vines to fullest maturity are the sweetest and juiciest of all. A sun-kissed tomato is sweeter than one grown under glass, although the flavor of a fully ripened greenhouse tomato is far superior to one that is picked when green or streaked with orange.

Shipped across state lines or imported from Chile and other places that celebrate summer when the rest of the world is suffering from winter doldrums, fresh tomatoes are available year-round. These tomatoes, often called "winter tomatoes," are grown not for their great flavor and juicy texture but for their ability to withstand the considerable rigors of transportation.

NUTRITIONAL VALUE
A medium-size tomato is high in potassium, and is a good source of vitamin A and a great source of vitamin C.

BUYING AND STORING
Choose unblemished, firm, and fully ripe tomatoes that yield to a little finger pressure and seem heavy for their size.

Vine-ripened summer tomatoes bursting with sweetness and flavor.

A hard tomato will not be juicy or flavorful. When buying tomatoes for sauces or ketchup, select overripe ones and cut away the few soft spots. Although there are special Italian paste (sauce) tomatoes, other varieties work equally well and have much more flavor. For snacking or decorating a salad, the smallest cherry tomatoes are an excellent choice. They also make wonderful sauce.

Some people seem to think it's necessary to peel tomatoes that are to be served in a salad. This is not the case for many of the varieties that are available at farm stands or fresh from the garden. The skins are a delicious part of the tomato and no tougher than the delicate skin of a sun-kissed peach. Unripe tomatoes taste sweeter when sliced, dipped in cornmeal, and fried. They are excellent for pickle and chutney recipes.

Do not refrigerate tomatoes unless they are overripe or have been sliced. Temperatures of 55° F and below interrupt the formation of the enzymes that control the development of flavor. Store ripe tomatoes in a bowl at room temperature away from direct sunlight. Also keep unripe tomatoes away from sunlight and hasten ripening by placing in a brown paper bag with an apple at temperatures between 65 and 75° F.

Freeze whole tomatoes for long-term storage. When ready to use, thaw and slip off the skins. Use the softened flesh in soups and sauces. When canning tomatoes, as a safeguard against botulism, the United States Department of Agriculture recommends filling the jars of raw, quartered tomatoes with boiling water and adding 1 tablespoon of bottled lemon juice or ¼ teaspoon crystalline citric acid per pint.

Change the accent of Swiss Tomato Pie by using cheddar, jalapeño, or blue cheese instead of Swiss.

PREPARATION

To top off a burger or layer on a sandwich, slice into a large beefsteak tomato. Large tomatoes also make ideal containers to hold a serving of chilled crab or tuna salad. They are also good for stuffing and baking. Or, much easier and just as tasty, cut in half and sprinkle with a mixture of chopped herbs, bread crumbs, and Parmesan cheese; drizzle with olive oil and bake. Medium-size tomatoes are the ones for cutting into slices or wedges and drizzling with olive oil and chopped fresh herbs. Or layer slices of red and yellow tomatoes with fresh mozzarella and basil leaves.

To skin a tomato, drop into boiling water for 20 seconds. Remove it from the water with a slotted spoon, spear the stem end with a sharp fork, and pull the skin off with a small, sharp paring knife. To seed a tomato, cut in half across the width and press gently to squeeze out the seeds or remove them with a small spoon.

To make tomato juice, take peeled and seeded tomatoes, quarter them, and place the quarters in a kettle. Bring to a boil, reduce heat, and simmer, covered, for 10 to 15 minutes. Puree cooked tomatoes in a blender or food processor. Season to taste with salt and pepper. Pour into airtight freezer containers and leave a ½-inch head space. Cover, label, and freeze. Or add 1 tablespoon of lemon juice to the hot juice and pour into hot, sterile canning jars. Leave a ½-inch head space, seal jars, and process in a boiling water bath for 35 minutes for pints and 45 minutes for quarts.

To stuff tomatoes, first cut the top (stem side) off a tomato and scoop out the flesh and seeds with a small, round spoon. If serving raw and stuffed with a mayonnaise-dressed filling, turn the hollowed tomato upside down to drain off some of the juices. When baking stuffed tomatoes, place in greased muffin cups to help them maintain their shape. Stuff with cooked rice, macaroni and cheese, or meat-and-bread crumb mixtures.

Fried Green Tomatoes

This is one of the tastiest ways to use up those end-of-the-season unripe tomatoes. Serve this dish for breakfast or dinner.

1	large egg
2	tablespoons skim milk
	Salt and pepper to taste
4	to **8** green tomatoes (depending on size), sliced ¼ inch thick
½	cup all-purpose flour
½	cup seasoned cracker crumbs
2	to **4** tablespoons vegetable oil

Beat the egg, milk, salt, and pepper together in a mixing bowl. Dip tomato slices in the flour, then into the egg mixture, and finally into the cracker crumbs. Heat 2 tablespoons of oil in a large heavy skillet over medium-high heat. When hot, add crumbed tomato slices to the skillet without overcrowding. Sauté the slices about 3 minutes a side until crispy golden brown. Remove to a plate and serve immediately or keep warm in a low oven. Repeat with the remaining 2 tablespoons oil and crumbed tomato slices.

Preparation time: 10 minutes
Cooking time: 6 minutes
Yield: 4 servings

Swiss Tomato Pie

This pie is so easy you'll wonder why you never made it before.

1	single 9-inch pie crust
6	large, firm, ripe tomatoes
	Salt to taste
6	ounces Swiss cheese, shredded or diced small (about 1½ cups)
1	large onion, finely chopped (about 1 cup)
¼	cup chopped fresh parsley
¼	cup chopped fresh basil leaves
	Pepper to taste
¾	cup sour cream

Roll out the pastry to fit a shallow, oblong baking dish. Pinch down the edges of the pastry with the tines of a fork. Refrigerate. Preheat the oven to 375° F.

Cut the tomatoes in half, scoop out seeds and juices (discard), and sprinkle with salt. Drain upside down. Combine the cheese, onion, fresh herbs, and pepper and spoon into the tomato halves. Place the filled tomatoes in the prepared pastry crust and spoon the sour cream over the top of each half. Place in the middle of the oven and bake 35 to 40 minutes, until the pastry and tomatoes are golden brown.

Preparation time: 25 minutes
Cooking time: 35 to 40 minutes
Yield: 6 servings

TURNIPS

BRASSICA RAPA, FAMILY CRUCIFERAE

Native to Europe, where it has been cultivated since Roman times, the turnip is grown for both its leaves and its root. Quick-maturing early turnips are small and white with thin skin and tender, crisp flesh. They may be globular, cylindrical, or a flat, round shape, and the colors may vary from pure white to white and purple. Late main-crop turnips take longer to mature. These are somewhat larger and, because they have thick skin, can be stored. Some varieties have yellow skin and flesh, while others have white and green skin with white flesh.

RUTABAGAS

BRASSICA NAPOBRASSICA

The rutabaga, a cross between a turnip and a cabbage, is said to have originated in Sweden during the late Middle Ages. For this reason, it is also called a Swedish turnip or Swede. Rutabagas have very hard, purple and yellow skin, and firm, yellow flesh that is very flavorful and sweet.

NUTRITIONAL VALUE

Rutabagas are twice as nutritious as turnips. One half-cup of cooked, cubed rutabaga provides 36 mg calcium, 244 mg potassium, 36 mg vitamin C, and 13.2 mcg folacin. Turnip greens win hands down, though, with their vitamin A and calcium content: a half-cup chopped raw provides 2,128 IU vitamin A and 53 mg calcium.

BUYING AND STORING

Turnips and rutabagas are available year-round from storage and fresh during the fall months. Store-bought rutabagas are likely to have a layer of wax.

Store in a cool, ventilated place for 2 to 4 months or in the refrigerator for up to 2 weeks.

PREPARATION

Young, tender, early-season turnips have a texture that is similar to radishes and are delicious when grated or sliced thinly and added to salads. Late-season turnips and rutabagas can also be slivered and eaten raw, but some people find they cause indigestion. For this reason, these main-crop roots are better eaten cooked, and can be added to soups, stews, casseroles, and soufflés. Cut into long "fingers," they can be roasted just like parsnips and potatoes. Diced and boiled, they are ready for tossing with butter and seasonings, mashing with potatoes (for the traditional Scottish dish of "neeps and tatties"), or chopping together with boiled carrots or parsnips. Tender turnip greens are pungently flavored and make a good substitute for spinach in either the salad bowl or as a cooked side dish.

Trim the turnip's tops and roots off, peel thinly, and cut large ones in quarters and small ones in half, then slice into 1-inch-thick strips or cubes. Boil or sauté in butter and pan liquids for approximately 15 minutes, until tender. To serve, chop them, mash them, or leave them whole.

To prepare rutabagas, cut a slice off the top and the bottom. On a cutting board, use a large, heavy kitchen knife to cut into the very hard flesh. Cut in half and then into quarters. Peel off the thick skin, then slice them thinly or dice them. Cook in a simmering soup for 20 minutes.

Stir-Fried Ginger-Mustard Turnips

2 *tablespoons olive oil*
1 *pound turnips, peeled and sliced ¼ inch thick and cut in ½ × 1-inch pieces*
2 *cloves garlic, minced*
2 *tablespoons grated ginger or* **1** *teaspoon ground ginger*
2 *tablespoons prepared mustard— spicy or sweet*

Heat the olive oil in a large skillet, add the turnip pieces, and sauté for 5 minutes. Add the garlic and ginger and sauté for 3 more minutes. Remove from the heat and coat with the mustard. Spoon into a dish and serve immediately.

Preparation time: 5 minutes
Cooking time: 8 minutes
Yield: 4 servings

Baked Turnips and Rutabagas

This is a wonderful combination of root vegetables. The rutabagas and carrots give color and flavor to the sweeter, milder turnips and parsnips.

¼	cup olive oil
1	pound rutabaga, peeled and cut in ½-inch-thick slices
1	pound parsnips, peeled and sliced ½ inch thick
1	pound turnips, peeled and sliced ½ inch thick
1	pound carrots, peeled and sliced ½ inch thick
6	cloves garlic, minced
½	cup chopped celery leaves
¼	cup chopped parsley
1	cup vegetable stock, vegetable juice, or water plus 1 bouillon cube
1	teaspoon ground nutmeg
	Salt and pepper to taste
1	cup fresh bread crumbs
½	cup chopped raw cashew nuts

Heat 3 tablespoons of the olive oil in a large skillet over medium heat and sauté the root vegetables for 5 minutes. Add the garlic, celery leaves, and parsley, stir to combine, then cook for 2 minutes. Combine the vegetable stock, nutmeg, salt, and pepper to the skillet and bring to a boil. Remove from the heat and spoon into a shallow baking dish. Preheat the oven to 375° F.

In a small skillet, heat the remaining tablespoon of olive oil and sauté the bread crumbs and chopped nuts for 2 minutes. Spoon over the vegetables and place the dish in the oven. Cook for 30 minutes, until the vegetables are tender.

Preparation time: 15 minutes
Cooking time: 40 minutes
Yield: 8 servings

Vary the flavor of Stir-Fried Ginger-Mustard Turnips by adding a drop of sesame oil and a little soy sauce.

In ancient times, herbs were appreciated for their fragrance and medicinal value. They were hung on doors to ward off evil spirits and placed on death beds to accompany loved ones into another world. Centuries ago, herbs were used to sweeten drinking water, preserve meats, mask bad flavors, and generally improve taste.

Although certain herbs complement particular foods, cooking with soft-stemmed annuals or woody-stemmed perennials to add a particular flavor is a matter of taste. What appeals to one cook may not appeal to another. What is more important is being able to recognize those herbs that are strong flavored, which can overpower delicately flavored foods like vegetables and fish.

Although some perennial herbs taste quite flavorful when dried, most of the annuals retain their best flavor when frozen or packed in oil. In fact, herbs frozen in oil retain the most flavor of all. When freezing or drying herbs, choose those with unblemished leaves or stems. If the plant flowers, the stronger volatile oils will be diminished in the leaves but will be concentrated in the flowers or seeds. When this happens, dry or freeze the flowers and cook the leaves. However, herbs such as basil, dill, cilantro, and anise still retain a strong flavor in their leaves if picked when the flowers are just opening.

DRYING HERBS

Collect herbs after it has rained but when the leaves are dry; this way you don't have to wash them. (Don't use pesticides, since herbs are rarely bothered by bugs or diseases. If they are, cut them off or pull them up and start again.)

If necessary, wash the freshly harvested herbs and either blot dry or use a salad spinner.

Tie a few sprigs together by the stems and hang upside down in a dark, airy cupboard or pantry. After about one week, check for dryness. When dry, strip off the leaves and store in a screw-top jar or a tin.

FREEZING HERBS

Wash, blot, or spin dry freshly harvested herbs and pack leaves and stems (or just leaves) into plastic freezer bags with the air pressed out. Freeze and use within three months.

Another method is to chop or puree the leaves (and very soft stems) with olive oil (2 cups leaves to ½ cup oil), then freeze them in half-cup or 1-cup containers. You can also pack the herb-oil mixture in ice cube trays and freeze it overnight, then remove from the trays and pack into plastic containers or freezer bags. Use for sautéeing, mixing with sour cream, tossing with hot vegetables, or adding to soups. When com-

bined with oil, herbs can be frozen for 12 months.

GROWING HERBS

All herbs like good drainage. Perennial woody-stemmed herbs will grow in rich, poor, sandy, or clay soils; soft-stemmed annuals (and perennials like sorrel and lovage) produce more luxurious leaves for a longer time when grown in humus-rich soil.

Pick out sturdy plants with new shoots or grow your own from seed. Annuals, in particular, are fast to grow from seed. Make sure they germinate after the last frost in your area or start them indoors on a sunny window sill.

Prepare a bed (raised, terraced, or mounded beds provide good drainage) in full sun or where the herbs will receive at least 6 hours of sun a day. By enriching the soil with organic matter, you won't have to use fertilizers during the entire season. Do not add lime unless you know your soil is acidic. Herbs do best when the soil has a neutral pH of between 6.5 and 7.5.

Plant on a cloudy day or in the evening and water well. Mulch with straw to keep weeds down (or make it easy to pull weeds out). When established and bushy, plants should be periodically cut back to prevent flowering and stimulate new growth.

You should seed fast-growing annuals (basil, cilantro, dill, chervil) every two to four weeks to keep the harvest coming on strong. Toward the end of summer, allow annuals to go to seed (when annual plants go to seed, it is their signal to end productivity) or just pull up. Mulch around perennials after the first frost.

SAUCES AND DRESSINGS

Sauces and dressings can work miracles for foods. Steamed vegetables, a bowl of plain rice, or pasta served unadorned does little to stimulate the appetite. Enhance the flavor of such simple dishes with the color and texture of sauces and dressings and they are immediately transformed into delicious appetizers or main meals.

The variations on sauces are endless. Change a basic white sauce by adding cheese, spices, herbs, or tomatoes. Or make sauces from pureed vegetables, low-fat buttermilk, yogurt, or light mayonnaise. Whir them in the blender or food processor and turn them into thinner dressings with the addition of a drop of olive oil and lemon juice or vinegar.

Vegetable Stock

1   *cup sliced celery*
1   *cup sliced carrots*
1   *cup sliced parsnips*
1   *cup sliced onions or leeks*
1   *cup tomato juice*

There is nothing easier than making a vegetable stock. Place sliced celery, carrots, parsnips, and onion in a 4-quart pot. Add tomato juice and enough water to cover the vegetables. Cover the pot, bring to a boil, and simmer for 1 to 2 hours. Strain the liquid into containers and discard the solid vegetables.

You can also make a delicious stock from whatever is going to waste in the vegetable bin. Just cut everything up small so that more surfaces are in contact with the water, throw in a handful of herbs from the garden, leftover scallion tops, zucchini, tomatoes, and anything else you have on hand, then let them simmer away while you go about your business. Strain, pour into containers, and freeze.

SAUCES

Classic White Sauce

2   *tablespoons butter, margarine, or vegetable oil*
2   *tablespoons flour*
1   *cup milk*
     Salt and pepper to taste

Melt butter in a saucepan. Stir in flour and cook this roux for 1 minute. Over medium heat, scald milk in a small saucepan and pour into the cooked roux, stirring all the time until the sauce is thick and smooth. Season to taste.

Microwave Method
Place butter in a 4-cup glass jug. Melt on high for 30 to 40 seconds. Stir in flour. Whisk in the milk until smooth. Cook on high for 2 minutes. Stir to combine and continue cooking for 3 minutes

longer, until thick. Remove and whisk smooth.

Low-Fat White Sauce

1½   *cups skim milk*
½   *cup nonfat dried milk (optional)*
2   *tablespoons all-purpose flour*
      Salt and pepper to taste

Pour 1¼ cups of the milk and the dried milk into a small saucepan and bring to a scald over medium heat. Make a smooth paste of the flour and remaining milk. Stir into the scalded milk and stir continuously to thicken to a creamy texture. Cook for 2 to 3 minutes. Season to taste.

Note: Substitute cornstarch for the flour if desired. However, the texture is not as stable as a sauce made with wheat flour. Increase the flour by 1 tablespoon for a thicker sauce.

SAUCES

White Sauce Variations
Use the following variations to flavor any plain white sauce.

Cheese   Add ½ cup of grated cheddar, blue cheese, and soft cheeses such as Brie or Camembert. Serve over cauliflower, broccoli, leeks, fennel, spinach, or other steamed vegetables.

Curry   Make a curry sauce by adding 1 or 2 tablespoons of curry paste or powder. Stir-fry celery, onions, summer squash, peppers, or broccoli and combine with the curry sauce. Serve over rice.

Mushroom   Sauté sliced mushrooms, add to the white sauce, and simmer for 5 minutes. Serve this creamy mixture over toast for breakfast, lunch, or a light supper.

Green Herb   Flavor the plain white sauces with 2 to 4 tablespoons of fresh chopped herbs. Parsley, dill, and chives are particularly suitable for combining with steamed carrots, lima or broad beans, leeks, celery, celeriac, Jerusalem artichokes, or potatoes.

Onion-Jalapeño Yogurt Sauce

This tastes good hot or cold. Serve it over broiled hake, haddock, catfish, orange roughy, or red snapper.

1	*tablespoon olive oil*
1	*medium yellow onion, chopped*
1	*fresh or canned jalapeño*
1	*tablespoon all-purpose flour*
½	*cup low-fat milk*
½	*cup plain yogurt*
½	*teaspoon ground coriander*
1	*tablespoon chopped cilantro*
1	*tablespoon chopped garlic chives*
	Salt and pepper to taste

Heat the oil in a skillet and sauté the onion over medium heat. Wear rubber gloves and remove the seeds from the jalapeño. Chop finely and add to the onion. Stir in the flour and cook for 2 minutes. Pour the milk into the mixture and stir constantly until it thickens. Remove this mixture from the heat and stir in the yogurt, herbs, and seasonings. Spoon the sauce into a bowl and serve immediately.

Yield: 1½ cups

Fresh Tomato Sauce

Serve this as a side dish or over tortellini or ravioli. For a heartier sauce to serve over spaghetti, add sautéed summer squash, peppers, celery, or eggplant. Or combine the tomato sauce with 3 to 4 cups of cooked beans (green or dried) and serve over rice.

1	*tablespoon olive oil*
1	*small onion, chopped*
2	*cloves garlic, minced or crushed*
5	*to **6** large tomatoes, peeled, cored, and chopped or **2** cups chopped canned tomatoes*
2	*tablespoons chopped fresh basil or **1** teaspoon dried basil flowers*
1	*tablespoon fresh oregano leaves or **1** teaspoon dried*
	Salt and pepper to taste

Heat the oil in a skillet and sauté onion over medium heat for 5 minutes. Add the garlic and cook 2 minutes. Add the tomatoes, herbs, salt, and pepper to taste. Cook 5 minutes, reduce the heat to low, and simmer, uncovered, for 10 to 15 minutes.

Note: Dried basil flowers are not commercially available. Dry your own between paper towels on the countertop. After several days, when dry, crumble into a bowl (do not cover) and place in a dark cupboard. This ensures thorough drying. After 1 week, place in a tin or jar with a screw top.

Yield: 2 cups.

Red Pepper Sauce

This sauce is delicious over vegetables, pasta, rice, or fish. It's also good spread on toasted French bread. Thin the sauce, if desired, with a tablespoon or two of sour cream or yogurt.

2	*tablespoons olive oil*
1	*medium red onion, chopped*
5	*large sweet red bell peppers, sliced*
2	*cloves garlic, minced or crushed*
2	*tablespoons chopped fresh parsley*
1	*tablespoon chopped fresh basil leaves or **1** teaspoon dried basil flowers*
	Salt and pepper to taste

Heat the oil in large skillet and sauté the chopped onion for 5 minutes over medium heat. Add the sliced peppers and garlic, then sauté for 10 minutes. Puree in a blender or food processor

Yield: About 4 cups.

Note: In place of the red peppers, use 5 cups sliced zucchini or sweet fennel.

From these simple ingredients it is possible to create a myriad of delicious sauces.

Cucumber and Yogurt Dressing

This has a very light and refreshing flavor and is delicious when spooned over thinly sliced young turnips, jicama, celery, sweet peppers, and other raw vegetables.

1   *large cucumber*
2   *cups plain yogurt or **1** cup yogurt and **1** cup low-fat sour cream*
2   *cloves garlic, crushed*
2   *tablespoons fresh chopped mint or **2** teaspoons dried crushed*
     Mint leaves to garnish

Peel and chop fine or coarsely grate the cucumber. Place in a colander lined with cheesecloth and allow to drain for 20 minutes. (A light sprinkling of salt draws out more liquid.) In a medium-size serving bowl, combine yogurt, garlic, and chopped mint. Twist the cheesecloth

around the cucumber and squeeze to get rid of the juices. Stir the drained cucumber into the yogurt mixture. Garnish with mint leaves.

Yield: About 2½ cups.

Ginger-Soy Dressing

This is a delicious dressing for shredded salads, Thai or Vietnamese fresh spring rolls, or stir-fried vegetables.

1   tablespoon plain or hot sesame oil (or to taste)
1   tablespoon grated fresh ginger
2   cloves garlic, crushed
1   teaspoon sugar
2   tablespoons rice wine or rice vinegar
½   cup light soy sauce (or tamari)
½   cup water

Measure all ingredients in a screw-top jar and shake to combine.

Yield: 1¼ cups.

Classic Vinaigrette

Use this dressing for steamed asparagus and leeks, hot potato salad, or any other vegetables. It gives great flavor to a salade Niçoise of crisp, steamed green beans, boiled cubed potatoes, sliced beets, tomato wedges, hard-boiled eggs, olives, and tuna fish.

¾   cup olive oil
¼   cup wine vinegar
1   clove minced or crushed garlic
1   tablespoon Dijon mustard

With practice it is possible to create a complementary dressing for any vegetable under the sun.

Combine all ingredients in a small bowl and whisk together until the mustard is suspended with the oil and vinegar.

Yield: 1 cup.

Low-Fat Vinaigrette

This dressing is not exactly oil-free, but it is lower in fat than the classic version.

⅓   cup olive oil or vegetable oil
⅓   cup mild, sweet vinegar
⅓   cup water
2   to 3 cloves garlic, crushed
1   tablespoon Dijon mustard
2   tablespoons chopped fresh herbs or 2 teaspoons of a salt-free spice mixture

Place all ingredients in a small bowl and whisk until thoroughly combined.

Yield: 1 cup.

Sesame Dressing

Try this dressing on raw or cooked, hot or cold vegetables. It's an all-around winner.

½   cup sesame paste
¼   cup creamy peanut butter
¾   cup plain yogurt
¾   cup light sour cream
2   large scallions, sliced
3   to 4 cloves garlic
¼   cup soy sauce (or tamari)
¼   cup toasted sesame seeds

Place all ingredients except for the sesame seeds in a food processor or blender. Puree until smooth. Spoon into a serving bowl and stir in the sesame seeds.

Yield: 2½ cups.

Note: If a thinner consistency is desired, add more yogurt, soy sauce, or a drop of water.

Yogurt Dressing

¾   cup plain yogurt
1   to 2 cloves garlic, crushed
2   tablespoons lemon or lime juice
2   tablespoons olive oil
2   tablespoons chopped fresh chives

Stir ingredients together in a small serving bowl.

Yield: 1 cup.

Note: Vary this basic dressing by adding 1 teaspoon curry powder, ½ teaspoon ground ginger, and 2 teaspoons honey; omit the chives and add 1 finely chopped shallot, 1 teaspoon paprika, and ½ teaspoon chopped hot chile pepper. For a milder sauce, replace half the yogurt with light mayonnaise. Unless homemade mayonnaise contains cooked eggs (raw eggs may contain salmonella bacteria), use store-bought mayonnaise.

PROP CREDITS

page 13—Artichoke Risotto: plate and wine glass, Williams-Sonoma.

page 18—Asparagus Stir-Fry: plate and fork, Pottery Barn.

page 22—Lima Bean Medley: plate and bowl, Pottery Barn; napkin, Williams-Sonoma.

page 25—Beet and Avocado Salad: plate and wine glass, Pottery Barn.

page 29—Broccoli Dip: platter and bowl, Platypus.

page 38—Kale and Kohlrabi: salt and pepper shakers, Williams-Sonoma.

page 45—Celery and Sweet Pepper Salad: green glass plate and green water glass, Pottery Barn.

page 64—Leeks Vinaigrette: plate and glass, Platypus.

page 68—Mushroom Stroganoff: plates and wine glass, Platypus.

page 83—Sugar Pea and Lettuce Soup: soup tureen and soup bowl and plate, Williams-Sonoma.

page 87—Couscous with Sweet and Hot Peppers: plate, yellow glass pitcher, and cup and saucer, Platypus; glass tumbler, Pottery Barn.

page 93—Praline Pumpkin Pudding: custard cups, Pottery Barn.

page 100—Cold Summer Squash Soup: plate, soup bowl, and napkin, Pottery Barn.

page 101—Zucchini cake: stand, cake plate, and dessert plates, Williams-Sonoma.

page 104—Sweet Potato Nut Bread: platter dish, Williams-Sonoma.

page 106—Swiss Tomato Pie: blue pie plate, Pottery Barn.

page 109—Stir-Fried Ginger-Mustard Turnips: blue plate, water glass, and cup and saucer, Pottery Barn.

Platypus: 128 Spring Street,
New York, NY 10012
212-219-3919

Pottery Barn: 700 Broadway,
New York, NY 10003
212-505-6377

Williams-Sonoma: 20 West 60th Street,
New York, NY 10022
212-980-5155